Anthropology's Ancestors

Edited by Aleksandar Bošković, University of Belgrade; Institute of Archaeology, Belgrade; Department of Anthropology, UFRN, Natal

As anthropology developed across geographical, historical and social boundaries, it was always influenced by works of exceptional scholars who pushed research topics in new and original directions and who can be regarded as important ancestors of the discipline. The aim of this series is to offer introductions to these major figures, whose works constitute landmarks and are essential reading for students of anthropology, but who are also of interest for scholars in the humanities and social sciences more generally. In doing so, it offers important insights into some of the basic questions facing humanity.

MAX
GLUCKMAN

● ● ●

Hugh Macmillan

berghahn
NEW YORK · OXFORD
www.berghahnbooks.com

First published in 2024 by
Berghahn Books
www.berghahnbooks.com

Library of Congress Cataloging-in-Publication Data

A C.I.P. cataloging record is available from the Library of Congress
Library of Congress Cataloging in Publication Control Number: 2024004314

British Library Cataloguing in Publication Data

A catalogue record for this book is available from the British Library

ISBN 978-1-80539-172-2 hardback
ISBN 978-1-80539-174-6 paperback
978-1-80539-463-1 epub
978-1-80539-173-9 web pdf

https://doi.org/10.3167/9781805391722

CONTENTS

• • •

FIGURES

• • •

ACKNOWLEDGEMENTS

● ● ●

I am grateful to Aleksandar Bošković for inviting me to write this short biography of Max Gluckman. Looking back over fifty years, I am grateful to P.H. Gulliver, Lionel Caplan, Eva Krapf-Askari and J.F. Morris (a lecturer in African law) for introducing me to the study of social anthropology when I did the MA Area Studies (Africa) in the first year that it was offered at the School of Oriental and African Studies (SOAS) in 1966–67. I majored in history with Professor Roland Oliver, who seemed very old to a twenty-one-year-old, though he was only forty-three, and with Shula Marks who was just beginning a distinguished career. Surprisingly, perhaps, I also attended lectures and seminars given by Professor Isaac Schapera, who had taught Gluckman at the University of Witwatersrand (Wits) in 1930, and by Dr Lucy Mair, who had helped to run Professor Malinowski's seminar, which Gluckman had attended at the London School of Economics (LSE) in 1934–36. I was also, through my mother, in touch at that time with Mary Douglas, who features in this book, and she introduced me to Victor Turner, who also features as a prominent member of the Rhodes-Livingstone Institute (RLI) and the Manchester School. Mary tried, without success, to persuade me to change from the study of history to social anthropology, but I like to think that she would be pleased to know that, through half-a-dozen learned articles and this short book, I have made a small contribution to the history of social anthropology.

I regret that I never met Max Gluckman, though I could have done, but I was introduced to his 'Analysis of a Social Situation in Modern Zululand' while doing this course at SOAS and I was able to discuss him and his work with my father, Professor W.M. Macmillan, who remembered him as a student at Wits in the early 1930s – they remained in touch until the 1950s – and with my mother, Mona Tweedie Macmillan, who remembered him from Malinowski's seminar, which she attended with many other anthropological luminaries in 1932–34.

My closest links with Gluckman came through his exact contemporary, fellow anthropologist and lifelong friend Hilda Kuper, and through Elizabeth Colson, who joined him at the RLI in Northern Rhodesia (Zambia) in 1946 and succeeded him as director of the institute a few years later, going on to work with him at the University of Manchester after that. I got to know Hilda well when I was working at the University of Botswana, Lesotho and Swaziland, in Swaziland (Eswatini), her area of special interest, in the 1970s. I visited her, and interviewed her and her husband, Leo, in Los Angeles in 1983. I met Elizabeth in Lusaka in 1978 when I joined the staff of the University of Zambia, and I remained in touch with her until her death in Zambia nearly forty years later. I am grateful to them both for what I learned from them about the history of social anthropology, and to Elizabeth especially for her input into, and generous comments on, my various anthropological papers from the 1980s to the 2000s. Other members of Gluckman's circle of friends to whom I was close included Lewis Gann, who I first met in 1962–63, Julius and Eleanor Lewin, who I first met in 1963, and Jack and Ray Simons, who I knew from 1969. Jack was a significant source for my early papers on the history of social anthropology and on Gluckman, as was Lewis Gann. I am also grateful to other members of Gluckman's circle, including Phyllis Deane, Ronnie Frankenberg, Iona Mayer and Colin Trapnell, who helped with my earlier research. I should also thank many other people who provided material or commented on my earlier papers. They include Andrew and Leslie Bank, Martin Chanock, Gervase Clarence-Smith, Daphna Golan, Karen Tranberg Hansen, Tom Johnson, Ivan Karp, Adam Kuper, Gwyn Prins, Paul Rich, Jeremy Seekings, Milton Shain, Leroy Vail and Megan Vaughan.

For recent help in the preparation of this book, I would like to thank Raymond Apthorpe and David Boswell, who agreed to be interviewed about their experiences in Zambia and Manchester, and Chris Hann, Karen Tranberg Hansen and Adam Kuper, who helped with comments and references. At the Royal Anthropological Institute, Sarah Walpole, Catherine Atkinson, Lavinia Cyrillos and Andrei Nkanu helped with the Gluckman archive and sourcing photographic material. James Peters provided information from Manchester University's archives. Elizabeth Cutmore helped at the SOAS archives and Lucy McCann helped, as always, at the Bodleian Library in Oxford.

The primary source for this book is the published work of Max Gluckman, but I drew on the work of many other authors. I should acknowledge, especially, Robert Gordon's massive biography, *The Enigma of Max Gluckman* (2019), the late Lyn Schumaker's *Africanizing Anthropology* (2001), which is important for the history of the RLI, and Seán Morrow's *The Fires Beneath: The Biography of Monica Wilson* (2016).

ABBREVIATIONS

* * *

ADR	alternative dispute resolution
BBC	British Broadcasting Corporation
CPGB	Communist Party of Great Britain
FISB	Federal Intelligence and Security Bureau
HMSO	His (or Her) Majesty's Stationery Office
KES	King Edward VII School, Johannesburg
NUSAS	National Union of South African Students
RAI	Royal Anthropological Institute, London
RLI	Rhodes-Livingstone Institute, Livingstone and Lusaka
SOAS	School of Oriental and African Studies
TLS	Times Literary Supplement
UDI	Unilateral Declaration of Independence
WENELA	Witwatersrand Native Labour Association
Wits	University of Witwatersrand, Johannesburg
WIZO	Women's International Zionist Organization

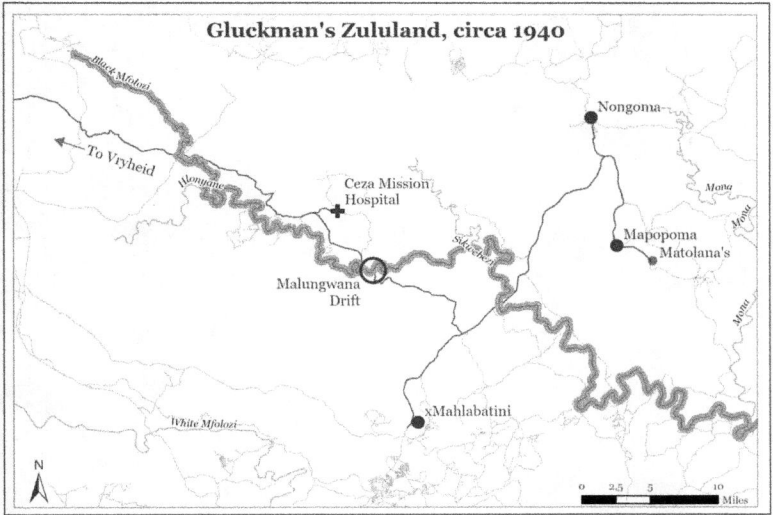

Gluckman's Zululand, circa 1940. © Philip Viljoen (simply maps)

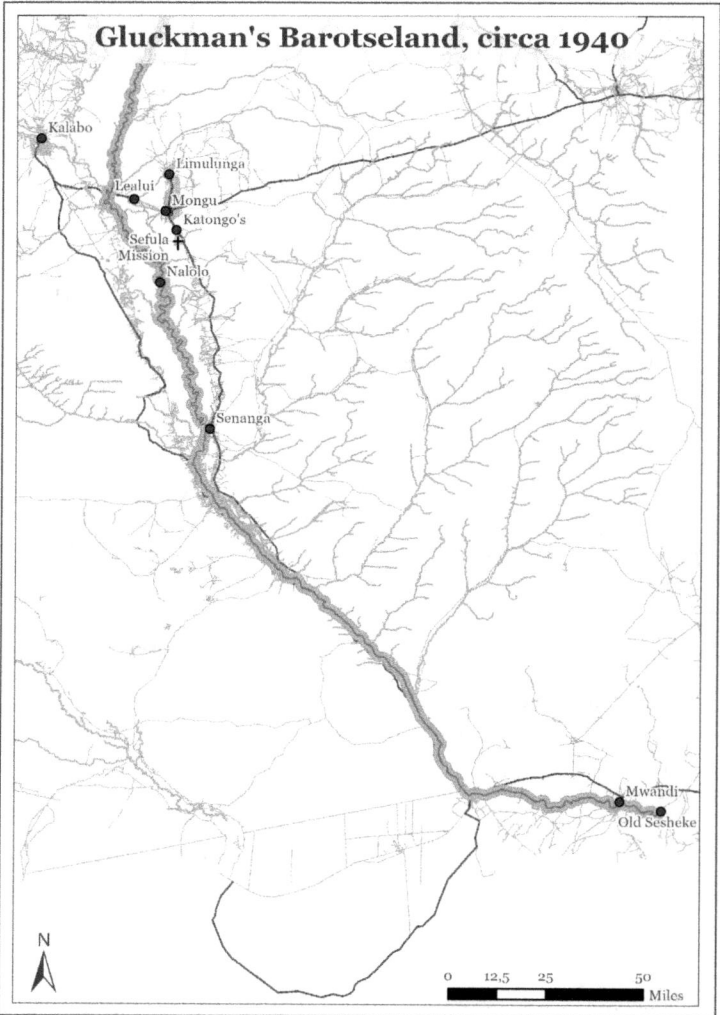

Gluckman's Barotseland, circa 1940. © Philip Viljoen (simply maps)

INTRODUCTION

• • •

Social anthropology achieved recognition as a standalone academic discipline in Great Britain and its Empire in the 1920s. It emerged out of anthropology, which had for long been seen primarily as a branch of natural history, with some input from classical and biblical studies. Leading figures in the development of anthropology included T.H. Huxley (1825–95), the evolutionary biologist, Sir Edward Tylor (1832–1917), a cultural evolutionist, William Robertson Smith (1846–94), a theologian and biblical scholar, and Sir James Frazer (1854–1941), the author of *The Golden Bough*, a classical scholar who coined the title 'social anthropology' in 1906 to describe 'a branch of sociology that deals with primitive peoples' (Kuper 2015, quoting A.R. Radcliffe-Brown). Social anthropology had to be distinguished from physical anthropology, cultural anthropology, ethnology, ethnography and sociology, though social anthropologists continued (and continue) to describe themselves, on occasion, as sociologists or ethnographers.

The two major figures in the emergence of social anthropology as a separate discipline were A.R. Radcliffe-Brown (1881–1955), a pupil at Cambridge of W.H.R. Rivers (1864–1922), a psychologist, and of A.C. Haddon (1855–1940), a zoologist turned ethnologist; and Bronislaw Malinowski (1884–1942), a Polish scholar who had studied mathematics and physics in Cracow, now in Poland, then in Austro-Hungary, as well as economics with Karl Bücher (1847–1930) and psychology with Wilhelm Wundt (1832–1920) at Leipzig in Germany. He moved to the London School of Economics (LSE) in 1910 to study with C.G. Seligman

(1873–1940), a pathologist turned ethnologist. Radcliffe-Brown did fieldwork on the Andaman Islands in the Indian Ocean and was appointed to the chair of social anthropology, the first such chair in the British Empire, at the newly established University of Cape Town in South Africa in 1921. He remained there until 1925, when he moved to the University of Sydney in Australia. After six years from 1931 at the University of Chicago, he became the first Professor of Social Anthropology at the University of Oxford in 1937. Malinowski did fieldwork on the Trobriand Islands, north of Australia, during the First World War. His was allowed to stay there for most of the war as an alternative to internment in Australia as a citizen of the Austro-Hungarian Empire and an enemy alien. He was appointed as a lecturer in social anthropology at the LSE in 1921. Regarded as the leading exponent of intensive 'fieldwork' and the convener of a famous seminar, he became a professor there in 1924, and moved to Yale University in the United States in 1939. Both Radcliffe-Brown and Malinowski were seen as exponents of 'functionalism', while Radcliffe-Brown created 'structural functionalism'. They were both interested in the functioning of social systems in the present and they were dismissive of the usefulness of history in the study of what they would both have described as 'primitive' peoples. They had a major influence on social anthropology as it was practised in Africa from the 1920s until decolonization in the 1960s.

Max Gluckman was the most influential of a group of social anthropologists, including Isaac Schapera (1905–2003), Monica Hunter (Wilson) (1908–82), Hilda Beemer (Kuper) (1911–92), Meyer Fortes (1906–83), Ellen Kaumheimer (Hellman and later Koch) (1908–82), Eileen Jensen (Krige) (1904–95) and Jack Krige (1896–1959), who emerged from South Africa during the 1930s into what was essentially a new academic discipline. Gluckman is best known today for his work on the ethnography and history of the Zulu of South Africa, and on the legal system of the Lozi of Northern Rhodesia/Zambia. His best-known work on the Zulu is his three-part 'Analysis of a Social Situation in Modern Zululand' (1940–2). In the context of the history of social anthropology, this was revolutionary in its focus on a single social situation or event (actually several events) occurring at a named place on a specific date with identified actors. His description and analysis of events in real time implied a rejection of contemporary social anthropological practice, of the 'ethnographic present' and of hypothetical or conjectural reconstructions, and an acceptance of the need to study 'primitive' societies in the context of the modern world. The underlying themes of conflict and cohesion remained central to much of his work. Asked to write an article on the Zulu for Edward Evans-Pritchard's (1902–73) and Meyer Fortes's *African Political Systems* (1940), he had become intrigued by the question of how such an intensely divided society as South Africa continued to function. He found his answer in what he later called 'the bonds in the colour bar'.

Gluckman's two monographs on Lozi customary law, *The Judicial Process among the Barotse* (1955) and *The Ideas in Barotse Jurisprudence* (1965), have remained highly influential. They sparked interest in the comparative study of legal systems and influenced the development of alternative methods of arbitration and dispute resolution in the United States, the United Kingdom and elsewhere. Gluckman became a public intellectual in the United Kingdom where he was a regular broadcaster on the BBC's Third Programme. He communicated some of his ideas on African society, and those of several of his contemporaries, to a wide audience through a series of broadcast talks, which were collected and published in *Custom and Conflict in Africa* (1956).

Gluckman was a member of the staff of the Rhodes-Livingstone Institute (RLI) at Livingstone in Northern Rhodesia/Zambia from 1939 to 1947, and was its acting director or substantive director from 1941 to 1947. He was Professor of Social Anthropology at the University of Manchester from 1949 to 1971, and head of the Department of Social Anthropology and Sociology from 1949 to 1965. He provided a personal and continuing link between these two institutions, at least until 1955, and his 'Analysis' became the foundation text of what was named by others as the 'Manchester School', an informal grouping of social anthropologists, mainly working on Africa, which emerged in the 1950s under his leadership.

CHAPTER 1

EARLY YEARS

• • •

FAMILY BACKGROUND

Max Gluckman was born in Johannesburg on 26 January 1911. He was a member of the third generation of his Jewish family to live in South Africa, but he was one of the first generation to be born there. His paternal grandfather had arrived with his family in the Transvaal Republic from Lithuania, then part of the Russian Empire, in 1896. He must have arrived with some capital, or rapidly accumulated it, as he was able to buy a farm and establish a mill near Potchefstroom. Max's father, Emanuel Gluckmann (Max dropped the second 'n' from his surname in the late 1930s), was born in Lithuania in 1881 and arrived in South Africa with his parents at the age of fifteen. He fought for the British during the Anglo-Boer War (1899–1902) and was able to study at the South African College (precursor of the University of Cape Town) after the war, reading law and graduating in 1906. He had married Katie Cohen in 1903, three years before his graduation – he was then twenty-two and she was nineteen. She had been born in Odessa, Ukraine, had come to South Africa as a child, and had grown up in the Western Cape. Max was the second of the couple's four children – three boys and a girl (Gordon 2018: 24–29).

As an immigrant Jew with liberal views on racial matters, it was not easy for Emanuel Gluckmann to establish and sustain a legal practice, and his financial status was usually somewhat precarious. He achieved some fame, or notoriety, by acting for the

Birwa, a Tswana 'tribe', in a case against Khama the Great, the veteran paramount chief or King of the Ngwato, in the British Bechuanaland Protectorate. The Birwa alleged maltreatment and violent dispossession. British colonial officials were protective of Khama and were frankly antisemitic and dismissive of Gluckmann, who published a pamphlet, *The Tragedy of the Ababirwa*, on the case in 1922. As a child, Max was conscious of his father's involvement in this case and, also, in the 1920s, in legal action in defence of Clements Kadalie, the Nyasaland-born leader of the Industrial and Commercial Workers' Union (ICU), the first Black workers' trade union. There can be no doubt that his father's involvement in, and suffering for, what would today be called 'human rights' cases had an influence on Max's later political views and intellectual interests (Gluckman 1971a: 373–74).

Max had less to say about the influence of his mother, Katie Gluckmann, but she was clearly an energetic and forceful woman who carved out a prominent place for herself in the Jewish community and the Zionist movement in South Africa. In 1928 she became the first woman to be elected to the executive of the South African Zionist Federation and became vice-chairman of the South African Women's Zionist Council on its establishment in 1932. She also became chairman of the South African branch of the Jewish National Fund in 1936 and was a formidable fundraiser. It may not be coincidental that South African Jewry became well known for the scale of its financial contributions to the international Zionist movement and also for the high proportion of its women who were members of the Women's International Zionist Organization (WIZO) (Shimoni 1980: 26, 29).

It does not appear that either of Max's parents was especially religious. Sir Raymond Firth (1901–2002), in an obituary notice written for the British Academy, summarized the relationship of Max and his family to Judaism and Zionism in these terms:

> He came from a non-religious background in South Africa, and himself was of fundamentally agnostic temperament. His parents respected Jewish religious custom and held a Bar-Mitzvah ritual for Max, though perhaps primarily for

social reasons. But the secular importance of Israel was very clear for them, and Max himself was proud of being Jewish culturally and socially – though he never really acquired any real knowledge of Hebrew. He visited Palestine in 1936 with his mother . . . and worked for a time in a kibbutz. (Firth 1975: 486)

The influence of Zionism on the family, mainly through his mother, was strong. Max was the only member of the family who did not move to Palestine/Israel either before or after the independence of Israel. He latterly supervised research on the country and, by chance, he died there, but he never lived there on a permanent basis. His elder brother Colin was a founder of Habonim, the Zionist youth movement, in South Africa in 1930 and emigrated to Palestine in 1936. He served in the paramilitary group Haganah and fought in the war of independence in 1948. He changed his surname to Gillon and, a lawyer by training like his father and both his brothers, became Israel's senior state attorney in 1952. Colin's son was for a while head of the Israeli security agency Shin Bet. Max's younger sister, Joyce Miller, moved to Palestine with her psychiatrist husband, Louis, in 1947, and his younger brother, Philip, also a founder of Habonim, moved to Israel with his family in 1951. Max's parents, Emanuel and Katie, moved to Israel in 1949 and died there (Gordon 2018: 28–29).

WITS

Max was educated in Johannesburg at King Edward VII School (popularly known as 'KES'), which had been founded in central Johannesburg by Lord Milner in 1902 as the Johannesburg College. The school was moved to Houghton Ridge in the northern suburbs and was renamed in memory of the British monarch soon after his death in 1910. 'KES' was a state school, but was modelled on the 'public' – that is, private – schools of England. Max was intellectually gifted, over six feet tall, and an all-round sportsman, excelling at cricket, football and, later, golf. He passed his matriculation or university entrance exams in 1927 at the age of sixteen with distinctions in all subjects and moved on to the University of the Witwatersrand (known as 'Wits') in the following year.

Wits had been established as a university in 1922, though arts teaching had begun at its predecessor, the Johannesburg School of Mines, which was located in the centre of the town, in 1917. The college moved from prefabricated buildings, known as the 'Tin Temple', in Jeppe Street, to a new and spacious campus in the suburb of Milner Park in 1923–25, and Max studied in the new buildings. The student body was, of course, almost exclusively white and predominantly English-speaking. A substantial minority of the students was Jewish and there was a smaller minority of Afrikaans-speakers. The university was both new and small, and there was a close relationship between staff and students. The arts faculty was seen as liberal, though there was a division within it between a few radical liberals, who believed in racial equality, and rather more liberal segregationists, who believed that Blacks needed protection from white competition. The political context from 1924 to 1929 was the drive of the PACT government – an alliance between Afrikaner nationalists and the English-speaking (and white) Labour Party, under the leadership of the nationalist Prime Minister, General J.B.M. Hertzog – for segregation. This was the predecessor of apartheid (Murray 1982: 39–92, 125–48).

Max registered in 1928, soon after his seventeenth birthday, for the ordinary BA as a necessary preliminary for a law degree, the LLB. According to the surviving transcript of the courses he took for the BA, he did logic as one of his first-year courses with the professor of philosophy, R.F.A. Hoernlé (1880–1943), who was an inspiring teacher with an international reputation, having taught in Britain and the United States, as well as in Cape Town. He had been appointed to the chair in 1923. He was regarded as a liberal and became President of the Institute of Race Relations after its establishment in 1929, but his book *South African Native Policy and the Liberal Spirit* (1939) provided aid and comfort to the advocates of apartheid through his statement that, though impractical, 'total separation' was the ideal solution to South Africa's 'Native problem'. Max's other first year courses were Chemistry I, English I, Geography I and Latin I.[1]

Hilda Beemer (later Kuper), a close friend from Max's school days, suggested on the advice of a friend that they should both do Social Anthropology I as a second-year course in 1929. It was taught by Agnes Winifred (known as Winifred) Hoernlé (1885–1960), wife of Professor Hoernlé. She had been appointed by Wits as a researcher in 1923, but only began to teach the subject after her appointment as a lecturer in 1926. Born Winifred Tucker in South Africa in 1885, she was the daughter of a mining surveyor who became Mayor of Johannesburg and, later, a member of the South African senate. After studying at the South African College in Cape Town, she won a scholarship to Cambridge, where she was taught by Haddon and Rivers. She also attended lectures by Sir James Frazer and A.R. Radcliffe-Brown. She moved on to Leipzig, where she studied economics with Wilhelm Wundt, and to Paris, where she attended lectures at the Sorbonne by Emile Durkheim, one of the founders of the new academic discipline of sociology. She did anthropological fieldwork, focusing on physical anthropology, with the Nama and San people in German South-West Africa in 1912–13. Following her marriage to Alfred Hoernlé in 1914, she moved with him to Boston in the United States, where she remained until 1920. On her return to South Africa, she met Radcliffe-Brown, then professor in Cape Town, who encouraged her to abandon physical anthropology and to work on kinship studies (Bank 2016: 15–63; Kuper interview 1983).

Winifred Hoernlé was not a great lecturer and did not publish a great deal, but she was undoubtedly a good scholar and an inspiring teacher who attracted several bright students, including Eileen Krige, Hilda Kuper, Max Gluckman and Ellen Hellman, to the new discipline. Hilda Kuper has left a comprehensive account of what was taught in the first-year social anthropology course, which they took in their second year of study. There were apparently twenty students registered for the course in 1926 and there may have been more in 1929, but according to Hilda, there were only four students, including herself, Max and Ellen Hellman, registered for the social anthropology major. They must have received a more intensive course of study than those registered for the minor (Hilda Kuper 1984).

Hoernlé sought to introduce her students to the different schools of anthropology. She began with the evolutionists and went on to the Austrian Kulturkreis school, whose leaders included Leo Frobenius (1873–1938), who visited Wits at this time, and Fritz Graebner (1877–1934), the German founder of the Vienna School of ethnologists, with whom she included the American diffusionists. This was followed by an introduction to the French school of sociology, with an emphasis on Durkheim, with whom she had studied. Hilda Kuper, who was also majoring in French, was given special responsibility for Durkheim. Gluckman was given responsibility for Sir Henry Maine (1822–88), author of *Ancient Law*, often described as the forefather of legal anthropology, and a significant influence on Max's later work; William Robertson Smith, pioneer of the comparative study of religion and of kinship studies; and the American ethnologist Lewis Henry Morgan (1818–81). They were also introduced to the work of other scholars, including Franz Boas (1858–1942), an early critic of scientific racism and an advocate of cultural relativism, on the Eskimos, and Henri-Alexandre Junod (1863–1934), missionary anthropologist and author of *Life of a South African Tribe*, on the Tsonga.

They were, of course, also introduced to Radcliffe-Brown and Malinowski's works on the Andaman and Trobriand Islanders, and to 'functionalism'. Its appearance on the intellectual scene has been dated to the publication in 1922 of Radcliffe-Brown's *The Andaman Islanders* and Malinowski's *Argonauts of the Western Pacific*. Hilda Kuper saw Malinowski and Radcliffe-Brown's adoption of 'functionalism' as a reaction against evolutionism and diffusionism (Kuper interview 1983).

Hilda Kuper claims that this was all taught in one year. Her account does differ in some ways from the outline included in the university calendar, and she may have conflated the first and second years. She also says that the select group of four students for the major took courses from Professor Raymond Dart (1893–1988), Professor of Anatomy at Wits from 1922, and co-discoverer in 1924 of 'Taung man', or *australopithecus africanus*, on physical anthropology; and from Clarence van Riet Lowe (1894–1956) on archaeology in the first year. Physical anthropology and archaeology were also taught to the honours students who did a third year of social anthropology.

In 1929 (his second year of study), Gluckman did a further three courses, Ethics I with Professor Hoernlé, Psychology I with Professor I.D. MacCrone, and Economics I with the youthful Dr S.H. Frankel (1903–96), who was promoted to professor in the following year at the age of twenty-seven. Gluckman later grouped MacCrone and Frankel with W.M. Macmillan (1885–1974), the Professor of History, as being the teachers at 'Wits' in the 1920s who saw South Africa as a single society, in marked opposition to the segregationist policies of the PACT government. Gluckman did not do the first-year course in history as a minor subject, as Hilda Kuper and her future husband, Leo Kuper (1904–94), did. However, he frequently acknowledged the influence of Macmillan, who was by far the most academically productive of the early Wit academics. He published four significant books, *The South African Agrarian Problem and Its Historical Development* (1919), *The Cape Colour Question* (1927), *Bantu, Boer, and Briton* (1929) and *Complex South Africa* (1930), and half-a-dozen pamphlets, between 1919 and 1930. Although Max may not have studied history formally, he may have attended some history lectures and became close to Macmillan, intellectually, politically and socially. They used to play golf together following the establishment of a university club in 1929 (Gluckman 1949: 5; Gluckman 1971a: 375, 405; Kuper interview 1983; author's personal knowledge).

Winifred Hoernlé went on sabbatical leave to London in 1930 and worked there with Malinowski at the LSE. She was replaced for the year by Isaac Schapera, who came up from Cape Town. He had studied social anthropology there with Radcliffe-Brown and had gone on to the LSE to work with Malinowski. He did not get on well with Malinowski and he transferred to C.G. Seligman for the supervision of his doctorate. Hilda Kuper, who was briefly engaged to marry Schapera, did not think highly of him as a lecturer, though she acknowledged the quality of his material. She recalled that you had to say to yourself: 'Don't go to sleep, what he is saying is good.' She was especially impressed by his lectures on law, 'which contrasted Radcliffe-Brown's emphasis on the different systems of law and the different types of sanctions with Malinowski's *Crime and Custom*, with its binding rules of reciprocity'. He seems, however, to have preferred Malinowski's approach (Kuper 1984: 196).

In the views of both Hilda Kuper and Max Gluckman, the most memorable event during Schapera's year at Wits was the expedition that he conducted to his fieldwork camp at Mochudi in the Bechuanaland Protectorate. Kuper was amused by the contrast between fieldwork as advocated by Malinowski, with its emphasis on participant observation, and Schapera's approach. He sat at a table and informants were brought to him. Gluckman was inspired to contribute an article on his first experience of fieldwork to *NUSAS*, the journal of the National Union of Students, which had been established in 1924. This article, which may have been his first published work, was entitled 'An Anthropological Trip: Visit to Native Reserve'. It is understandably immature, but the trip did lead him to agree with 'psychologists and anthropologists who consistently maintain that there is no difference in the innate mental endowment of the various races of mankind'. He concluded by recommending that all South Africans should 'visit the native reserves, and they will clearly realise of the Kaffir, that he is a man, fit to take part in the up-building of the greater South Africa' (quoted in Gordon 2018: 37).

Gluckman and Kuper both completed their BA degree at the end of 1930 and graduated early in the following year. Apart from Social Anthropology II, Max's other third-year courses were Logic II, with Professor Hoernlé, and Zulu I, with Professor Clement Doke (1894–1980), whose original expertise was in Northern Rhodesian African languages, but who became an expert on Zulu linguistics. While Kuper went on to do the honours course in 1931, Gluckman began the LLB and did law courses in

1931 and 1932. The law faculty was not strong. A Scots professor, R.G. McKerron, had been appointed in 1926 at the age of twenty-six – Scots law and Roman-Dutch law having an affinity – but almost all the teaching was done by part-timers. Some of those with whom Gluckman may have had contact, including Oliver Schreiner (1890–1980) (nephew of the novelist Olive Schreiner) and W.H. Ramsbottom (1895–1961), went on to have distinguished careers as appeal court judges (Murray 1982: 192–93).

Max returned to social anthropology to do the honours course in 1933, graduating with a first-class degree, the only one that Mrs Hoernlé ever awarded. In addition to coursework, the honours degree required the writing of two long essays – mini-theses. His essay 'Zulu Women in Hoe Culture Ritual' was published in *Bantu Studies* in 1935 as his first academic publication, and he also wrote 'A Comparative Study of the Economic Position of the Chiefs in Certain Southern Bantu Tribes'. The writing of these two long essays, especially the first of them, may help to explain how he was able in 1934–6 to write a massive dissertation for his Oxford D.Phil. in less than two years – the first of them was incorporated into it.

Gluckman entered the third year of the LLB in January 1934, but he did not complete it. He was awarded a Rhodes Scholarship for the Transvaal, and moved to Oxford in time to begin the academic year there in October 1934. Not long before his departure for Oxford, he had been introduced in July by Mrs Hoernlé to Malinowski in Johannesburg during his visit for the New Education Fellowship conference. The two lectures he gave on that occasion on 'Native Education and Culture Contact' were published in 1936 and provided an almost perfect rationale for 'Bantu Education' as it was introduced by the Nationalist government in the early 1950s. 'Natives' should only be given a level of 'schooling' that suited their inferior status in South African society. Like Professor Alfred Hoernlé in his later book, Malinowski had revealed himself to be a 'liberal segregationist' (Macmillan 1989: 82–84).

The award to Gluckman of a Rhodes Scholarship came as recognition not only of his academic excellence, but also, as the terms of the scholarship required, of his all-round achievements as a sportsman, representing the university at football, cricket and golf, and as a student leader. He was chairman of various student societies and the editor of, and a frequent contributor to, several student newspapers. He contributed what Robert Gordon describes as a 'scathing editorial' to *WU's Views* on 3 June 1932 on the report of the Native Economic Commission Report, to which several Wits staff, including Macmillan, Frankel and the Hoernlés, had given evidence. This followed a meeting at Wits on 31 May, which was addressed by F.A.W. Lucas, a member of the commission. A lengthy and critical intervention by Macmillan after Lucas's address seems to have had a lasting impact on Gluckman. His editorial concluded:

> Let us set our own house in order and stop worrying about the ultimate effect on our children in hundreds of years to come, as Professor MacMillan [*sic*] says, they will thank us more for that. (Quoted in Gordon 2018: 38)

Almost forty years later, Gluckman recalled the decisive influence of Macmillan's intervention on his own single most influential contribution to social anthropology: 'Analysis of a Social Situation in Modern Zululand' (1940). Writing in an autobiographical essay in 1971, he recalled:

> I was, and am, fully aware of the extent to which white and African oppositions dominate the South African system, indeed increasingly so since the 1930's, as shown in the movement from the policy called segregation to that of apartheid. But the experience that influenced, and influences, my presentation of these principles in analysis was hearing Professor W.M. Macmillan, the great historian who first brought Africans and their societies into proper perspective in historical analysis,[2] say: 'If people worried about the next ten years, instead of the next fifty years, there would be some hope for South Africa.' This taught me that to look into the distant future, or to examine a soci-

ety at its highest levels of order and oppositions, distracted
important attention from immediate, short-run problems.
It might well be that at some time in the future differential
incorporation of the ethnic groups must produce, under
the principle of the developing dominant cleavage, violent
disturbance and radical change. In the immediate present
my duty as a scientist was to try to understand how the system worked, and was likely to continue working, at least in
the short run. Thirty years later it still works. (Gluckman
1971a: 375–76)

In a letter to his future wife Mona Tweedie written on 1 June
1932, Macmillan left his own account of his 'mighty outburst',
which had such a long-lasting impact on Gluckman. He, incidentally, hinted at some of the underlying tensions between history and anthropology, which were then current at Wits. These
were to surface later in the critique of 'functionalism', which was
mounted by South African anthropologists, including Gluckman,
Schapera, Kuper and Monica Wilson – but especially Gluckman.
Macmillan wrote:

The Report is forever making it all the blacks' fault and put-
ting up special pleading to justify their own [the authors']
and the Europeans' caution. I couldn't be content to have
a university audience (a lot of my best pupils) led in the
way of caution, and I revolted against their carrying on with
politic gratitude for the positive advance which the Report
is. So I let them have it for twenty minutes, and know it
went well.

The main point was that instead of self-justification and
complacency they would get nothing done until they sub-
stituted a white sheet of *repentance*. I gave them chapter and
verse from the report and pricked a lot of bubbles. With
Mrs. Hoernlé at my side I had to be gentler than I meant to
be with the anthropologists, but went bald-headed at the
absurdity of two civilisations,[3] and told them the Africans

would do their own adaptation. Went on to insist on the importance of 'the discontented minority' as the Report calls them, i.e. the progressives who *will* produce the leaders, either with us or against us. I finished as usual by reminding them that there is some more of Africa, and told them the real meaning of indirect rule. (W.M. Macmillan to Mona Tweedie, 1 June 1932, quoted in Macmillan 1975: 219)

For Macmillan, 'the real meaning of Indirect Rule' was that British colonial governments were trying to use so-called 'traditional leaders' where they existed and to invent them in stateless societies where they did not, as a means of tame local government. Their intention was to stifle the emergence of the 'progressives', an educated African middle class, into local and, later, national government. He saw social anthropologists, with some justification, as the colonial government's allies in this pursuit and was to develop this argument in his book *Africa Emergent* (1938).

In his biography of Gluckman, Robert Gordon (2018: 54, 95) suggests that two authors (Paul Cocks and Hugh Macmillan) have greatly exaggerated (Gordon 2018: 54, 95) Macmillan's influence on Gluckman and have underestimated the influence of his true 'mentor' J.D. Rheinallt Jones (1884–1953), a founder in 1922 of the Johannesburg Joint Council of Natives and Europeans, and in 1929 of the South African Institute of Race Relations. Given his 1971 testimony, quoted above, where Macmillan is mentioned twice (at 374 and 405), and his numerous other references to Macmillan and his work, including one in the 'Analysis' and no less than three in *An Analysis of the Sociological Theories of Bronislaw Malinowski* (1949: 2, 5, 13), it is difficult to see how his influence has been exaggerated.[4]

Gluckman was, of course, close to Jones through his involvement in the Pathfinders, a racially segregated version of the Boy Scouts for African boys, which Jones had established in 1922 – his wife, Edith, set up the Wayfarers, a version of the Girl Guides, for African girls. Gluckman had been a Boy Scout at KES and became a District Pathfinder Master while at Wits. He continued to correspond with Jones after he left Wits, and Jones wrote some

Figure 1.1. Max Gluckman in uniform as a Pathfinder (scout) master, Johannesburg, circa 1934. © RAI. 400.155993

references for him. Gluckman may have done Jones's course on Native Law and Administration, as Gordon suggests, but there is no evidence that Jones had any intellectual influence on him. Jones was an energetic organizer and a part-time lecturer in the Bantu Studies department, which was set up in 1926, but he had no academic qualifications and was neither an academic nor an intellectual. Hilda Kuper described him as 'a very funny man' who habitually dressed in Pathfinder uniform. He became a Native representative senator in 1937 and was latterly a labour adviser to the Anglo American Corporation (Gordon 2018: 40, 54; Kuper interview 1983).

It was around the time of the Native Economic Commission debate that Gluckman became actively involved in student politics at Wits, and nationally through the National Union of

South African Students (NUSAS). He became a member of the Students' Representative Council (SRC) in 1932 and was a Wits delegate to the NUSAS students' parliament in 1932, 1933 and 1934, latterly as leader of the Liberal group. In 1933 he encouraged Phyllis Lewsen (later a professor of history at Wits) and H.C. Nicholas to propose that the South African Native College at Fort Hare, then South Africa's only tertiary education institution for Black (African, Cape Coloured[5] and Indian) students, should be invited to join NUSAS. After prolonged debate, a commission was established with Gluckman as chairman to consider the question. He later recalled that it was then 'that I learnt of the intransigence of most of the Afrikaner intellectuals on African questions: eventually I had to resign, because I could not work with the Afrikaner members, and I would not compromise'. This was one of the issues that contributed to the secession from NUSAS in 1934 of the Afrikaans-language universities and to the formation of the separate Afrikaanse Nasionale Studentebond. Fort Hare was not admitted to NUSAS until 1945 (Gluckman 1971a: 374).

OXFORD

Gluckman moved to Oxford in time for the beginning of the academic year – Michaelmas term – in October 1934. He had tried to have the scholarship transferred to the LSE, which would have been a better place to study social anthropology and where he could have worked with Malinowski, but that was impossible as the Rhodes Scholarships had to be held at an Oxford college. He became a member of Exeter College, which had an anthropological connection. The rector (head of the college) was Dr R.R. Marett (1866–1943), who had been appointed to a university lectureship in anthropology in 1910. Marett was an ethnologist and an exponent of the evolutionary school of cultural anthropology. His primary interest was in the anthropology of religion, which may explain why Gluckman chose, as the topic of his doctoral dissertation, 'The Realm of the Supernatural among the South-Eastern Bantu'. This was a surprising subject for a man who, according to his later colleague Elizabeth Colson, always said that he had a 'blank spot' about religion (Macmillan papers, Elizabeth Colson to Hugh Macmillan, 29 March 1996). It is of course possible that he discovered this deficiency during his research for the dissertation. The doctorate, which was the first Oxford D.Phil. awarded in social anthropology, did not require fieldwork and Gluckman's dissertation was library-based.

Given his disappointment at not being able to transfer his Rhodes scholarship to the LSE, Gluckman was fortunate that Oxford was only an hour away from London by train and he was able to travel up every Thursday to attend Malinowski's seminar, which he did for five terms in 1934–36. He later observed that the one day a week that he spent in London, often spending the night there, was more intellectually stimulating than the other four working days he spent in Oxford. He got to work quickly, presenting a paper on the role of the chief in relation to the 'tribe' in South Africa to the seminar in mid-November 1934. He provided a conventional description of South Africa with its two main climatic zones, the high-rainfall and warmer coastal areas, and the drought-prone and cooler inland areas. Emphasizing the similarity of the social and political structure in the two regions with governance through chiefs, councils and headmen, he pointed to the role of the chief as trustee of the land, with responsibility through his subordinates for its distribution, and to the importance of first-fruit ceremonies, in which the chief played the leading role, for the timing of the harvest. He also pointed to the chief's control of the timing of the harvesting of grass and reeds for thatching. During the discussion of the paper, it was pointed out that his account of the South African political system was limited by the inadequacy of the secondhand material on which it was based. More information was needed on the real sources of the chief's power and on the workings of the economic system, which was centred on the chief. More information was also required on the negative sanctions and positive inducements that led people to obey their chief (Macmillan papers, 'Seminar, Thursday, 15th November 1934. Discussion on material by M. Gluckman', Mona Tweedie (Macmillan)'s copy).

Gluckman may not have learned much from his elderly super-visor Dr Marett, but he undoubtedly did learn a great deal from Edward Evans-Pritchard (1902–73), usually known as 'E.P.'. A student of Seligman, he had already done extensive fieldwork on the Azande and the Nuer in Sudan. He was living in London, but he came to Oxford once a week to teach in the Anthropology Department from October 1935 onwards. He introduced Gluckman to Meyer Fortes (1906–83), who was his senior by a few years, and a South African with a similar Lithuanian Jewish background. He had studied at the LSE with Seligman and Malinowski. These three scholars were to remain lifelong friends, though in the case of 'E.P.' and Gluckman, there were some later ups and downs in the relationship.

Max appears to have written this two-volume, 732-page and roughly 200,000-word dissertation in not much more than eighteen months. He began work in October 1934, submitted the dissertation in May 1936 and it was examined in June. It emerged as a comparative study of 'the realm of the supernatural' in three peoples: the Thonga of Mozambique, the Zulu of Natal and a group that he (oddly) described as 'the Transkei'. This was not a comparable ethnic group, but was a reference to the isiXhosa/isiPondo-speaking people of the Transkeian territories, now part of the Eastern Cape. His only source for the Thonga was Junod's massive two-volume book *The Life of a South African Tribe*, which he described as 'magnificent'. His main sources for the Zulu were the published and unpublished works of Father A.T. Bryant, then attached to the Department of Bantu Studies at Wits, Eileen Krige's dissertation on the Zulu, which was published as a book, *The Social System of the Zulus*, in 1936, and both published and unpublished work by two serving Natal colonial officials, H.C. Lugg, and H.T. Braadvedt. He also used Magema Magwaza Zuze's *Abantu Abanyama Lapa Bavela Ngakona* (1922), his only historical source in an African language. His major source for the Transkei was the unpublished manuscript of Monica Hunter (Wilson)'s work on the Pondo, which was published in 1936 as *Reaction to Conquest*. He also used two books, *The South-Eastern Bantu* (1930) and *Ama-Xosa Life and Custom* (1932) by James

Henderson Soga (1860–1941), the mixed-race son of the Reverend Tiyo Soga and his Scottish wife, Janet Burnside, as well as the late nineteenth-century publications in German of the lexicographer of the isiXhosa language Dr Albert Kropf, and books by two members of the Brownlee family. He referred to information gathered from Ben Ngaba, a caretaker in Johannesburg, on the Gaika (Ngqika) of the Transkei – his only African oral source. He also acknowledged two books by Dudley Kidd, *The Essential Kafir* (1904) and *Savage Childhood* (1906), which did not relate to a clearly defined South African 'tribe' (Gluckman 1936).

Gluckman cited some publications by Malinowski, Marett and Radcliffe-Brown, and referred to rather more books by his teacher and friend Isaac Schapera on the Tswana. He cited fourteen publications, more than any other author, by Evans-Pritchard, on the Azande of the Sudan/Congo. The important book *Witchcraft, Oracles and Magic among the Azande* by 'E.P.' was not published until 1937, but Gluckman had access to his articles and unpublished work, which influenced his interpretation of religion and magic. He also used information from Meyer Fortes on the Tallensi of the Gold Coast, later Ghana. He may have been enabled to work as quickly as he did on the dissertation because he had studied Junod's work for the ordinary BA at Wits, and he had written a long essay on the hoe-culture ritual of Zulu women for the honours degree.

The bulk of the dissertation consists, as Gluckman himself acknowledged, of 'description *ad nauseam*' (ix) of 'minor details' of the ritual behaviour of what he defined as the South-Eastern Bantu 'culture area'. He concluded that this was a homogeneous culture area, though there were some differences between the Thonga and the other groups. He acknowledged that these differences may only have become apparent as a result of the quality and intensity of Junod's study.

In his introduction, Gluckman stated: 'I realise that the study of ritual is the most difficult of all studies of primitive behaviour' (i) and he referred to the earlier work of Tylor, Frazer, Marett, Durkheim and Lévy-Bruhl. He also acknowledged that the publication of Radcliffe-Brown's work on the Andaman islanders in

1922 was a great step forward in the study of ritual, as was, to a lesser extent, the publication of Malinowski's book on the Trobriand islanders in the same year. He took issue, however, with Malinowski, whose work on science, magic and religion demonstrates 'the fallacy of attempting to deduce sociological theories from the study of a single society'. He did not show 'how Trobriand mystical beliefs operate reasonably in accord with objective reality'. This is something that, he claimed, Evans-Pritchard does for the Azande.

Gluckman stated that he was going to attempt a survey of South-Eastern Bantu beliefs and a sociological description of ritual, something that 'had not yet been attempted for an African culture area' (xxiii). He stated that: 'One of the fundamental problems which I wish to consider is the way in which the savage, guided absolutely by empirical knowledge in some things, will exclude the knowledge in others.' His emphasis here would be on 'social situations'. He would compare social situations in one culture and between cultures. He noted that 'one is inevitably faced with the nature of primitive mentality, with the relation in the savage's mind of magic, religion and empirical knowledge'. He hoped to pursue the problems raised during these enquiries during his forthcoming fieldwork among the Zulu (xxv–viii).

After some brief introductory chapters, a 200-page chapter on 'ritual in social and individual life' provides a comparative survey of rituals associated with birth, initiation, marriage, death and the afterlife. A chapter on 'leechcraft' deals with medical practice and another 200-page chapter deals with 'ritual in economic life', including hoe-culture ritual, first-fruits ceremonies and harvest rites, cattle magic, as well as hunting and fishing ceremonies. A chapter on 'national life and law' deals with warfare and ceremonies of chieftainship. There is also a short chapter on 'wizards, magicians, and Gods'. A longer chapter deals, as he had promised, with the classification of 'modes of ritual behaviour': magic, ancestral cult, and what he defines as 'substantive' and 'factitive' ritual – the 'functioning' of ritual. The dissertation ends with a short comparative survey of ritual in the culture area.

Although it was common practice among social anthropologists in the 1930s, it is a little surprising, for someone with apparently liberal and progressive views, that Gluckman uses the ethnographic present and makes no reference at all to the facts of conquest and colonial rule. He frequently refers throughout the dissertation to 'primitive man' and, following Lévy-Bruhl (1857–1939), Radcliffe-Brown and Evans-Pritchard, to 'primitive mentality' or the 'savage mind'. He also refers, anachronistically, to the Xhosa as 'Kaffirs', though he quotes J.H. Soga, who refers to them more properly as the 'Ama-Xosa'. Referring to the divide between psychology and social anthropology, he emphasizes that he is a social anthropologist who knows nothing of psychoanalysis, and has not been psychoanalysed, but he states, a little puzzlingly, that:

> Freud and his followers have proved a remarkable similarity between the thought of the psychotic[6] and the mystical notions of a primitive man, and there must be some reason for this. (xx)

Gluckman also poses what he describes as 'another psychological problem': whether or not the similarities in the South-Eastern Bantu are due to biological inheritance, noting that they are 'of common stock, living in similar environments'. He refers to history only in terms of its anthropological schools, the 'much-abused' English school, whose exponents included E.B Tylor, W.H.R. Rivers and Grafton Elliot-Smith (1871–1937), and the American school, including Franz Boas, Paul Radin (1883–1959) and Robert Lowie (1883–1957), which he prefers.

The 'Analysis', which Gluckman published four years later, could hardly have been more different. He had, by then, abandoned the ethnographic present, he engaged with present time, and real history, and he had nothing to say about 'primitive mentality' or the 'savage mind'. Only the emphasis on the importance of 'social situations' seems to have made the transition from one piece of work to the other. This change can, perhaps, be explained by the impact of fieldwork. He had in his dissertation acknowledged that he was doing things the wrong way around – fieldwork should have come first. But his marriage, and a new exposure to Marxism, also had an impact.

THE ZULU

Almost as soon as Gluckman had finished his D.Phil., he set off for South Africa to do two years postdoctoral research among the Zulu. He would return to Oxford for the third year of his Rhodes Scholarship in 1938–39. Although he had glowing references from Mrs Hoernlé and others, he had been unable to get funding for this research from the London-based International African Institute, which was suffering from financial stringency. He did, however, get an initial grant of £300, not a very large amount for two years' research, from the South African Council on Social and Educational Research (Carnegie Fund). This was dispensed by E.G. Malherbe and he received a further £400 in the second year.

By his own reckoning, Gluckman spent sixteen months in 1936–38, doing fieldwork, intermittently, in northern Zululand. His father lent him a large American car and he travelled from Johannesburg by way of Swaziland, where he visited Hilda Kuper, to Nongoma, the magistracy and unofficial capital of northern Zululand, arriving there in October 1936. Acting on the advice of the Native Commissioner at Nongoma, E.N. Braatvedt, an expert on Zulu history and a friend of Mrs Hoernlé, he established himself at the homestead of Chief's Deputy Matolana Ndwandwe, thirteen miles from Nongoma and three miles from Mapopoma's trading store. Matolana was the Zulu King's representative in the Kwadabazi (Mapopoma) subdistrict. He was one of the King's most important advisers and was entitled to try civil cases. He had been employed on the gold mines as a 'boss-boy', earning £10 a month, and he sometimes complained that his official duties went unpaid. Following the death of King Solomon ka Dinuzulu in 1933, the place of the King was held by a regent, Prince Mshiyeni ka Dinuzulu, Solomon's brother, acting on behalf of Solomon's young son and heir, Cyprian, who was to become King in 1948. The South African government did not at this time officially acknowledge the Zulu Kingship and it only recognized Prince Mshiyeni as acting chief of the royal Usuthu 'tribe'. Gluckman required the permission of both Prince Mshiyeni and H.C.

Figure 1.2. King's representative Matolana Ndwandwe, Gluckman's host in Zululand, listening to a court case, circa 1937. © RAI. 400. 032714

Lugg, the chief native commissioner for Zululand, to live in the reserve and to do his fieldwork.

He originally pitched his tent at Matolana's, but soon moved into a hut – normally a council meeting room – in the homestead. He paid five shillings a month in rent and he also undertook to provide Matolana with sugar and tobacco, and lifts in his car, which were certainly of greater value. He employed Richard Ntombela, a relation of Matolana's, and a Christian, who lived half a mile away, as a servant, and he sometimes employed Zulu clerks for secretarial work. He had done two years of isiZulu language at Wits, but he was not a great linguist and, according to at least one white observer, a veterinary officer, he did not speak the language well (John Wright in conversation, quoting his father, F.B. Wright). He did, however, get by, and his lack of fluency did not prevent him from trying to live as a Zulu. He adopted Matolana's surname, Ndwandwe, and, on occasion, wore a *bheshu*, a man's animal-skin buttock-covering. His attempt to live like a 'Native' caused disquiet to some observers, both Black and white, and contributed to the problems he experienced when he sought to return to the field in Zululand in 1939. In the posthumously published chapter of his manuscript, 'Conflict and Cohesion in Zululand', written in the 1940s, he gave a frank account of his relationship with the people at Matolana's and the suspicion with which he was generally viewed:

> My behaviour here in which I seemed to give more that I got, for they could never see what I gained from watching their ceremonies or taking texts from them . . . heightened their suspicion. For what White gives something to Blacks without expecting a return at great interest? 'Whites treat Blacks as they do fish. At first they throw meat into the water and the fish eat it. It is good. The next day there is a hook in it.' 'Who would pay you just to study?' The mass of Zulu, to the end I fear, regarded me as *ifokisi* (a Government spy or detective) and there were complaints to the Paramount Chief Mshiyeni, because he had so much to do with me. I am sure that a lurking fear that this was my work remained even in the minds of the people of Kwadabazi, Matolana's sub-district, where I lived and worked longest and where there was real affection between myself and many of the people. Many challenged me time and time again about my business. When I first arrived, a popular thesis was that I planned to open a store and was smoothing the paths of my investments by giving gifts to the people. Others thought that I was going to become a missionary and was first learning, like many other missionaries, their customs. (Gluckman 2014: 183–94)

The people also had great difficulty in placing Gluckman in any one of the four ethnic stereotypes – English, Boer, Jew or German – which they normally used to classify white people. He noted that he 'fitted into no stereotypical position, politically, functionally, economically, racially, religiously' and was regarded as eccentric. He soon, however, made friends and his hut resumed its former role as a meeting place where men came to drink and philosophize. He became 'an accepted figure at law sessions, weddings, beer drinks' and at the cattle dip.

Gluckman expressed gratitude to Matolana and his people who had enabled him to spend 'many happy months' with them. He became known as 'Matolana's White' or *umlungu wakithi* (our white man). He specifically denied, however, that he was 'adopted' or that he 'went Native'.

Gluckman travelled widely in Zululand in 1936–38, often accompanying, or providing transport for, Prince Mshiyeni and members of his family as the Regent went about his duties. It was not until 1939 that he was officially recognized as the acting paramount chief – though not the king – of the Zulu. Gluckman would dearly have liked to live with Mshiyeni at his royal headquarters, but the latter made it clear that there was no question of that. He realized that Mshiyeni had a difficult job, caught as he was between officials of the Native Affairs Department, the representatives of the white state, the demands of labour recruiters for the mines and the Zulu people, who were increasingly divided between Christians and 'pagans', modernizers and 'traditionalists'. Furthermore, many people suspected him of wishing to usurp the throne and take it from his nephew. Gluckman sympathized with him as he attempted to run 'a state within a state torn by internal conflicts', but he thought that he himself also needed sympathy as he sought to maintain a friendly relationship with him. He noticed that Mshiyeni sometimes reacted angrily to what he thought were intrusive questions, and he felt that it was almost inevitable that there would eventually be a serious clash.

The crisis occurred when Gluckman drove some of Mshiyeni's councillors to a large meeting of 6,000 people that he was holding at Vryheid in Natal in November 1937, about eighty miles from Nongoma. The purpose of the meeting was to enable Mshiyeni to report back on the first session of the Natives Representative Council, to which he had been appointed. This council had no power and was described by African nationalists as the 'toy telephone'. It had been set up in terms of the segregationist legislation of 1936, which had abolished the common-roll franchise for Africans in the Cape. Mshiyeni stayed at the depot of the Native Recruiting Corporation (NRC). On the evening before the meeting, a drunken man insulted Mshiyeni who was visiting an NRC official at his house at the depot, saying: 'You know nothing.' Soon afterwards, apparently in retaliation, a prince and an induna attacked the offender with *sjamboks* (cowhide whips).[7] The NRC official, who did not speak Zulu, asked Gluckman to intervene. He restrained the induna, while the secretary of the Zulu Cultural Society, who was also present, restrained the prince. Gluckman then handed the offending drunkard to the NRC official, who expelled him from the yard.

It soon became apparent that Mshiyeni was highly offended by Gluckman's action. He had promised to introduce him to the crowd at the meeting, but when Gluckman took his councillors to the meeting, as agreed, he did not do so. Matolana, fearing that his own relationship with Mshiyeni was being 'spoiled' by the behaviour of his guest, begged Gluckman to apologize. He initially refused to do so, believing that he had acted correctly, but he eventually did so for the sake of his friendship with Matolana. He made the first approach to Mshiyeni and they shook hands on the matter. It appeared that peace had been restored, but news of the clash soon spread, and this affected Gluckman's standing in Zululand and his local relationships. He was able to continue his fieldwork, but he heard later that Mshiyeni had asked the native commissioner, presumably Braatvedt, to remove him from his district. He was not then removed, but the commissioner, demonstrating the difficulty of Gluckman's position, told him that if he had not intervened to stop the flogging, he would have removed him on that account.

Gluckman described his fieldwork and this incident, which occurred just over a year after his arrival in Nongoma and rather more than halfway through his fieldwork, in great detail. He saw his description as demonstrating 'the interplay of conflict and co-operation between personalities and groups', which underlay his later analysis. He suggested that:

We are all involved day by day in events arising out of the ethnic heterogeneity of the Union which affect our earnings, our standard of living, our ideas of justice and morality, our status as members of colour groups, even our personal safety. (Gluckman, 2014: 191)

RETURN TO OXFORD

Gluckman returned to Oxford for the third and final year of his Rhodes Scholarship for the academic year beginning in October 1938. This year was to be important for three reasons: he met and married Mary Brignoli; through his wife, he had greater exposure to Marxism and communism than before; and he came under the influence of A.R. Radcliffe-Brown, who had become Oxford's first Professor of Social Anthropology in the previous year.

Gluckman met Mary Brignoli on a skiing holiday in Switzerland with a group of Oxford students in Switzerland on New Year's Eve 1938. They became engaged four months later and were married in June 1939. Mary was the orphaned daughter of an Italian lawyer and an English actress, and had attended Wycombe Abbey, a prestigious girls' public school. She was no longer an Oxford undergraduate when she met Max in 1938 because she had, as a second-year student at Somerville College studying modern languages, been 'sent down' – that is, expelled – in October 1937. She had been found in her boyfriend's out-of-college room and was reported to the college by his landlady. This became something of a *cause célèbre* because the boyfriend was 'rusticated' – suspended for a term – while she was permanently excluded. This was in spite of a petition signed by many members of Somerville College's junior common room, including a newly arrived first-year undergraduate, Indira Nehru (Gandhi), later Prime Minister of India, which protested against their inequitable treatment (Frank 2002: 118; Gordon 2018: 162–64).

Mary was the beneficiary of a trust fund, but she joined the Communist Party of Great Britain in 1937 and remained a member until 1952, although with a break while she was in Northern

Rhodesia from 1939 to 1947.[8] She had attended the World Youth
Congress in New York State in August 1938 and was a member
of its youth secretariat. She was also involved in helping refugees from Nazism to leave Czechoslovakia. There is debate as
to whether Gluckman himself ever joined the Party. Mary told
Daphna Golan that he did join, while Hilda Kuper was certain
that he was never a member. Jack Simons (1907–95), on the
other hand, a leading member of the Communist Party of South
Africa from 1937 until its dissolution in 1950 and, like Kuper, a
close friend of Gluckman, said that he was 'probably a member'
of the Party when he wrote the 'Analysis' in 1939–40. Elizabeth
Colson (1917–2016), Lewis Gann (1924–97) and Peter Worsley (1924–2013) were among those who thought he was never
a member. The probability is that he was a member, but only
briefly. He told John Barnes in Oxford in 1947–48 that he was no
longer a member. He complained to him about the tedium of the
compulsory 'party prayer meetings' that he had to attend when
he was a member. The implication is that he had been a member,
with Mary, in 1938–39, but that, unlike her, he had not rejoined
on their return to the United Kingdom in 1947 (Barnes 2007: 285;
Gordon 2018: 162–64; information from Daphna Golan; Macmillan papers; Hilda Kuper to Hugh Macmillan, 8 October 1985;
Jack Simons to Hugh Macmillan, 21 July 1993).

The question of whether Gluckman was, or was not, a card-carrying member of the Party would be academic if this was not a
rumour that haunted him for twenty years and resulted in the
Australian government excluding him from Papua New Guinea
in 1960. That decision was apparently based, somewhat absurdly,
on information from MI5 and/or the Federation of Rhodesia and
Nyasaland's Intelligence and Security Bureau (FISB) that he had
joined the British Communist Party in 1951 – the year before
Mary, by her own account, resigned. There can be no doubt,
however, that he was, through Mary, close to the Party and influenced by Marxism from the late 1930s to the early 1950s (Gray
2019: 59–76).

Gluckman worked closely with Radcliffe-Brown, Evans-
Pritchard and Meyer Fortes in Oxford in 1938–39. It was at this

time that Radcliffe-Brown and Fortes were laying the foundations
of what emerged as 'structural functionalism'. Radcliffe-Brown
held seminars in his rooms at All Souls College, and he was especially interested in structures and systems. With Fortes and
Evans-Pritchard, he was engaged in compiling the edited collection that appeared as *African Political Systems* in 1940.[9] Gluckman
contributed a thirty-page chapter on the Zulu to this volume –
'The Kingdom of the Zulu of South Africa' (Gluckman 1940, in
Fortes and Evans-Pritchard 1940: 25–55). The chapter provides
a fairly straightforward account of the Zulu kingdom as it was
in two periods, under King Mpande and under colonial rule. He
later thought that the most significant contribution of the article
was his identification of the Zulu kingdom as subject to a cycle
of rebellions aimed at the replacement of the king, but never of
revolutions that would replace the institution (Gluckman 1963:
8). It was while working on this chapter in Oxford in 1938–39
that he formulated the questions relating to conflict, cohesion
and equilibrium that underlay his 'Analysis' – an essay that he
wrote, while staying with Godfrey Wilson in Livingstone, Northern Rhodesia in September/October 1939.

The possibility that Gluckman might join the staff of the
Rhodes-Livingstone Institute (RLI), which was established as a
centre for social and archaeological research in central Africa in
Livingstone in 1938, was first raised with him by its first director,
Godfrey Wilson (1908–44), in February 1938. Gluckman, who
was at Nongoma, expressed interest, but said that he would have
to finish his work on the Zulu first. The process of recruitment
turned out to be long, complicated and politically fraught. Wilson's preferred candidate was Meyer Fortes, but he was aware that
the trustees of the institute, who included conservative representatives of the British South Africa Company, would prefer a candidate of 'pure-bred British stock'. Fortes withdrew his application,
interpreting this requirement as antisemitic, and the job was offered in turn to two or three candidates with Anglo-Saxon names,
including Louis Leakey (1903–72), who later achieved fame as a
palaeontologist. These candidates all dropped out and Gluckman,
though South African and Jewish, was offered the job of Assis-

tant Anthropologist a few days after his marriage in June 1939, and he accepted it. He had references from Radcliffe-Brown, Evans-Pritchard and Fortes, as well as E.N. Braadvedt. The understanding was that he, as the second social anthropologist to be appointed to the RLI, would do fieldwork among the Lozi people in the Barotseland protectorate, a separate entity within the boundaries of Northern Rhodesia, in what is now western Zambia (Morrow 2016: 166–68; Gordon 2018: 174–78).

All these negotiations had been going on under the shadow of a world crisis and the complications did not end there. Max and Mary travelled by ship to South Africa in August and then went on by train over 1,800 miles from Cape Town to Livingstone, arriving in Northern Rhodesia a few days after Great Britain declared war on Germany, and entered the Second World War, on 3 September 1939. Gluckman's response to the outbreak of war seems to have been a little confused. On the one hand, he is said to have welcomed the Nazi-Soviet Pact in August, as many (though not all) communists did, and to have initially opposed the war. On the other hand, he sought in September to be released from his contract with the RLI – he had not yet started work – so that he could join the armed forces. He was apparently unable to do that in Northern Rhodesia as he was disqualified by his age and South African citizenship (Gordon 2018: 178).

Gluckman's reinstatement with the RLI was not entirely straightforward and it was at this moment that he sought permission to return to the field in Zululand. The result was a flurry of correspondence in October/November 1939 involving Mrs Hoernlé, Douglas Smit, the Secretary for Native Affairs in Pretoria, H.C. Lugg, the Chief Native Commissioner for Natal, a long-time critic of Gluckman, E.N. Braatvedt, the former Native Commissioner at Nongoma, who had recommended him for the RLI job, and Braatvedt's successor as commissioner in Nongoma, M. Langfield, who interviewed Prince Mshiyeni on the subject. All the old issues, including the incident at Vryheid, were brought up. Mshiyeni said bluntly that he did not like 'Europeans who want to live in Native Kraals' – 'I do not want him here'. He commented:

He is always asking people how they are treated, if they are over-taxed, whether they are oppressed, and whether the Chiefs and Indunas like the feeling of being under European rule. I think he is working for someone undisclosed. In fact, the man may be a communist whom we are warned against.

Mshiyeni's questions were also, at times, 'too intimate regarding our sexual life'. He suggested that Gluckman should be allowed to 'worry' some other district. (Langfield to Lugg, 9 November 1939, quoting Mshiyeni, National Archives, Pretoria, NTS 53/378, quoted in Macmillan 1995: 42).

Smit told Mrs Hoernlé at the end of November that Gluckman would not be allowed to return to the field in Zululand. This decision, although a great disappointment, was by then largely redundant, as he had already begun fieldwork in Barotseland. He had, however, been writing his 'Analysis of a Social Situation in Modern Zululand' during this period of global crisis and personal crisis in September/October 1939, and there can be no doubt that his personal experience of conflict with both the modern and 'traditional' authorities in Zululand had an impact on what is arguably his single most influential piece of academic work (Macmillan 1995: 41–43).

NOTES

1. Max Gluckman's course record card for the BA appears to have been misplaced, as Robert Gordon, in researching his biography, was unable to access it. He believes that Gluckman's first year at Wits was 1929, not 1928, as it was. The historian of Wits, the late Bruce Murray, had access to the course record and forwarded its contents to me in an email on 23 March 2012. In outlining Max's courses here and below, I draw on that source.

2. Gluckman included a footnote reference here to Macmillan's *Bantu, Boer, and Briton* (1929).

3. This is almost certainly a reference back to Radcliffe-Brown's inaugural lecture in 1923 when he had said that South Africa was 'faced with

a problem of immense difficulty and great complexity . . . the need of finding some way in which two very different races, with very different forms of civilization, may live together in one society' (Radcliffe-Brown 1923: 141).

4. Ronald Frankenberg was present when Macmillan addressed the Manchester seminar in circa 1952. He notes: 'W.M. Macmillan's demeanour and age inspired respect without any prompting; Gluckman introduced him with awe and admiration' (Frankenberg 2005: 182).

5. In South Africa some, though not all, people of mixed-race descent self-identify as 'Coloured'. The Cape Coloured People are a distinct ethnic group.

6. 'Psychotic' was replaced by 'neurotic' in this context and attributed to Freud in a later article. See Gluckman 1944b: 32.

7. The assault was carried out by 'a prince' and an induna (Gluckman, 2014: 190) and not, as Robert Gordon suggests, by 'the prince', Mshiyeni (Gordon 2018: 110).

8. She gave these dates in an application for an American visa in 1957. Application quoted in Foreman (2014: 44).

9. For recent commentary on the significance of this book, see Lewis (2022).

CHAPTER 2

'ANALYSIS OF A SOCIAL SITUATION IN MODERN ZULULAND'

• • •

Although the title of Gluckman's article refers to 'a social situation', it actually refers to two events and several situations that he witnessed on the same day of 7 January 1938.[1] On that day he rose at dawn and drove with Matolana, and his servant, Richard Ntombela, from Mapopoma's to the Mahlabatini district to attend the opening of a new low-level bridge over the Black Umfolozi River at the Malungwana Drift. They went on to attend a magisterial district meeting at Nongoma in the afternoon, and he returned home at 10 pm. The new bridge carried a branch road from the Durban-Nongoma main road to the Ceza Lutheran Mission hospital. The bridge had been funded through the Native Land and Trust legislation of 1936. The ceremony was attended by H.C. Lugg, the Chief Native Commissioner of Natal (CNC), Prince Mshiyeni ka Dinuzulu, the Regent of the Zulu Nation, Chief Mathole (father of Chief Mangosuthu Gatsha Buthelezi), the local chief and head of the Buthelezi clan, and various other white officials, missionaries and hospital staff, traders and labour recruiters, Zulu dignitaries and local people. The crowd included about twenty-four Europeans, including the wives of some officials, and about 400 Zulu, including the labourers who built the bridge. Among those present were two of Gluckman's school friends, L.W. 'Ronnie' Rossiter, the Government Veterinary Officer (GVO), and J. Lentzner, a member of the Native Affairs Department's engineering staff (Gluckman 1958: 2–4).

Gluckman provides a richly detailed and a decidedly 'functionalist' account of the proceedings at the bridge, pointing to the different roles of the participants, to the elements of European and Zulu culture that were combined in the ceremony, and to the incidence of racial separation. He describes how he travelled to Nongoma in his own car together with his servant and Matolana, but that they had to have breakfast separately at the hotel. On their return from the bridge in the GVO's car, they again had lunch separately at the hotel. He also describes, and provides a map to show, the distribution of the Black and white groups, and the Black subgroups, such as 'pagans' and Christians, at the ceremony. He also details the interactions between Black and white participants and summarizes the speeches of the major protagonists, the Chief Native Commissioner and Prince Mshiyeni (Gluckman 1958: 5–7).

Gluckman takes three pages to describe the event at the bridge, but only one page to describe the meeting at Nongoma in the afternoon, where the Nongoma magistrate and Native Commissioner Braatvedt, and, once again, Prince Mshiyeni were the leading actors. While the ceremony at the bridge brought together Black and white people in a communal celebration, the meeting at Nongoma related to conflict – faction-fighting – within one of the three major Zulu groups: the Usuthu, the Amateni and the Mandlakazi. It was the latter group that was called to order by the magistrate and by Prince Mshiyeni (Gluckman 1958: 7–8).

After his descriptions of the two events, Gluckman introduced his analysis in these words:

I have presented a typical example of my field-data. It consists of several events which were linked by my presence as an observer, but which occurred in different parts of Northern Zululand and involved different groups of people. Through these situations, and by contrasting them with other situations not described, I shall try to trace the social

Figure 2.1. Gluckman's photo of Zulu men crossing the new bridge over the Malungwana Drift to greet the Chief Native Commissioner (CNC) H.C. Lugg and Zulu Regent Mshiyeni, 7 January 1938. This photo was used to illustrate the 'Analysis', *Bantu Studies*, 1940. © RAI. 400.032705

> structure of modern Zululand. I call them social situations as I am contrasting them with other situations in the social system of Zululand. (Gluckman 1958: 8–9)

Gluckman went on to insist that the fact that Zulu and Europeans could cooperate in the celebration at the bridge demonstrated that 'they form together a community with specific modes of behaviour to one another'. He felt obliged to insist on this point because Malinowski had in his introduction to a then recently published collection of essays on 'culture contact' taken issue with Schapera and Fortes for adopting an approach that he (Gluckman) had forced upon him by his material. In a frequently quoted passage, Schapera had written that 'the missionary, trader and labour recruiter must be regarded as factors in tribal life in the same way as are the chief and magician' (Schapera 1938: 189).

Figure 2.2. Gluckman's photo of H.C. Lugg speaking at the opening of the new bridge, 7 January 1938. Left to right, standing: Lugg, Matolana Ndwandwe, interpreter Mkize, Regent Mshiyeni and a Zulu policeman. Photo also used to illustrate the 'Analysis', *Bantu Studies*, 1940. © RAI. 400.032701

Gluckman insisted that 'the existence of a single African-White community in Zululand must be the starting point of my analysis'. He could, he wrote, 'speak of "Zululand" and "Zululanders" to cover Whites and Zulu, while "Zulu" connotes Africans alone' (Gluckman 1958: 9–10).

Gluckman provided a detailed description of the event at the bridge in which he explained why everyone was there and what their role or function was. He noted that those present were divided into two colour groups – Zulu and European – and 'their direct relationships were mostly marked by separation and reserve'. Socially enforced separation could, however, be 'a form of association, even co-operation'. In a vital passage, emphasizing the impossibility of segregation, he noted that the 'schism between the two colour-groups is itself the pattern of their main integration into one community. They do not separate into groups of equal status: the Europeans are dominant. The Zulu could not, save by permission as domestic servants making tea, enter the White group's reserves, but Europeans could more or less freely move among the Zulu, watching them and taking photographs, though few chose to do so' (Gluckman 1958: 12–13).

Gluckman noted that the 'economic integration of Zululand into the South African industrial and agricultural system dominates the social structure. The labour flow includes practically all able-bodied Zulu; at any moment about one-third of the men in Nongoma district are away at work'. He also noted that 'in the labour centres the Zulu rub shoulders with Bantu from all over Southern Africa, and, though their Zulu nationality involves them in fights with men of other tribes, they come to participate in groupings whose basis is wider'. These included trade unions in which the Zulu could participate with other African, Indian, Coloured and even white workers 'in situations distinct from those which demand tribal loyalty'. He anticipated future conflict between the trade unions and the chiefs.

Zulu opposition to government, whether through chiefs, trade unions or the churches, was largely ineffective because of the government's monopoly of force. The government tended to attribute opposition to the modern equivalent of the witchcraft accusation – the alleged influence of communist propaganda. The political and economic dominance of Europeans over Zulu, 'as capitalists and skilled workers on the one hand, and unskilled labourers and peasants on the other,' (Gluckman 1958: 17) could be paralleled in other countries, but in Zululand there were distinctive features, which enhanced the separation between the groups. These included political and ecological differences, which were emphasized by differences in 'race',[2] colour, and language. 'The Zulu desire for the material goods of the Europeans, and the Europeans' need for Zulu labour, and the wealth obtained by that labour, establishes strong inter-dependent interests between them. It is also a potent source of their conflict' (Gluckman 1958: 19).

In the latter section of the first of his three articles, Gluckman examined in great detail the differences between the colour groups, but also the differences within them. He examined the

Figure 2.3. Gluckman's photo of Zulu warriors, singing the *ihubo* and leading the cars carrying the CNC and the regent back over the newly opened bridge, 7 January 1938. Photo used to illustrate the 'Analysis', *Bantu Studies*, 1940. © RAI. 400.032706

divisions within the Zulu as between 'tribes', lineages and homesteads, and between Christians and 'pagans'. He looked at the differences within the European group as between officials, traders and missionaries, but also at the contradictions within and between the colour groups. Zulu Christians sometimes identified with white Christians; white officials sometimes identified with 'their' people, as did white missionaries. He also noted that while the Zulu were generally opposed to the government, they showed remarkable – and, to him, puzzling – loyalty to it in the context of the Second World War, which had broken out in September 1939.

Gluckman noted that the apparently harmonious gathering at the bridge was 'a feature of relations between Zulu and Whites in Reserve territory which would not easily occur in European farm areas or in towns, where the conflicts between the groups are greater' (Gluckman 1958: 24). He summed up the situation at the bridge by saying that:

the groups and individuals present behave as they do because the bridge, which is the centre of their interests, as-
sociates them in a common celebration. As a result of their
common interest they act by customs of co-operation and
communication, even though the two colour-groups are
divided according to the pattern of the social structure . . .
By comparing the pattern of this situation with many other
situations we have been able to trace the equilibrium of Zululand social structure at a certain point of time.

Gluckman concludes that 'the superior force of the White
group . . . is the social factor in maintaining this equilibrium'
(Gluckman 1958: 25). But he also noted that the dominant situations were rapidly becoming 'those involving African-White
relations, and more and more Zulu behave as members of the African group opposed to the White group. In turn, these situations
affect *intra*-African relations' (26).

The second of Gluckman's articles – 'Social Change in Zululand' – is largely historical. He states his objective as being to
examine some of the historical processes, which had, over the
preceding 120 years, produced the contemporary equilibrium.
The first section, covering the emergence of the Zulu nation
from the late eighteenth century and the development of a 'Zulu-
White community' from 1824 to 1887, culminated with the Zulu
War of 1879 and the subsequent civil war. It drew largely on the
published work of Father A.T. Bryant. In a footnote added to the
1958 edition, he emphasized that by using the word 'community', he had not meant 'to convey that Zulu and White formed
an harmonious, well-integrated lot of people, but a lot of people
co-operating and disputing within an established system of relations and cultures' (Gluckman 1958: 35, fn. 1).

The second section, from 1887 (the date of the British occupa-
tion of Zululand) to 1906, was largely based on Gluckman's own
work on the records of the Nongoma magistracy in the Natal archives, to which he had somewhat restricted access until the latter date. This covered important events such as the imposition on
Zululand in 1891 of the Natal Legal Code, which deprived chiefs

of criminal jurisdiction, and it concluded with the Bambatha Rebellion. He emphasized, as he had done previously, that 'Force established White rule and the threat of force maintained it . . . The threat of force remains one of the dominant factors in the Zululand equilibrium' (42). However, it was 'money rather than the Maxim gun, or telephone, which established social cohesion, by creating common, if dissimilar, interests in a single economic and political system, though it is one with many irreconcilable conflicts'. The integration of Zulus and whites into a single system had proceeded rapidly (Gluckman 1958: 42–43).

Although the main emphasis of this article was historical, it also dealt with the contemporary situation – 'the development of the modern Zululand equilibrium' – and made some remarkably accurate observations about the emergence of what would come to be called 'traditionalism'. Gluckman noted that:

> Some better educated Zulu tend to return to the old customs and this seems a turning back; it is encouraged by Government as part of the policy of segregation and parallel development, and has produced a social anthropology which records the vitality of Bantu culture without reference to its causes. This vitality may be ascribed to an attempt to bridge the gap between Christians and pagans, to the revulsion of the educated Zulu from the White civilization they are denied, and to the politically safe means it offers of expressing Zulu pride and hatred of the culture to which they dare not aspire. (Gluckman 1958: 44)

Gluckman was clearly aware of the movement among the Natal *amkholwa* (Christian converts) that had led to the founding of Inkhata, a cultural organization, in 1924 and of the Zulu Cultural Society in 1937. He was also aware of the tendency towards the aggregation and expansion of the influence of Zulu ethnicity. At the same time that opposition to government had been heightened, there was increased allegiance to chiefs and, especially, to the Zulu kingship, even in areas of Natal and the Transvaal, which had not formerly been under its control. Anticipating the later arguments of David Cannadine about the British monarchy, he noted that: 'Sentiment about the king grows, helped by his lack of power, because he has no power to abuse' (Gluckman 1958: 67; Cannadine 1983: 101–64)

Although Gluckman had used historical research to establish points of stable equilibrium in the past, he had not entirely escaped the anti-historical influence of Malinowski and Radcliffe-Brown, and he was anxious to point out that he was not trying to identify a 'zero-point' against which to measure social change. He claimed, a little contradictorily, that he had been able to explain the modern equilibrium without reference to its history. 'Historical material was not needed to understand the pattern of the system' (Gluckman 1958: 44). He followed Fortes in emphasizing that it was necessary to study 'communities rather than customs'.

'SOME PROCESSES OF SOCIAL CHANGE'

The third article in the 'Analysis' – 'Some Processes of Social Change' – was published in *African Studies* in 1942, two years after the first two. It was the most ambitious and, in the view of some contemporary readers, the most ambitious and/or pretentious, and, almost certainly, the least successful of the three articles. Responding to the suggestion that sociology was not scientific because it did not produce replicable laws for social change, Gluckman sought to 'formulate abstractly processes of social change' – 'invariable relations between events in changing social systems' (Gluckman 1958: 52). He distinguished between two classes of social systems – repetitive systems, such as the Zulu kingdom before the arrival of the Europeans, and changing systems, such as Zululand after their arrival.[3] Looking at culture, he distinguished between the way that people see their own culture, which he defined as *endoculture*, and the way in which culture is seen by other members of the same social system, which he defined as *exoculture* (54–57). Although he elaborated his arguments with many examples from the Zulu kingdom and

Zululand, it cannot be said that his ideas in this article had any significant impact, either at the time or subsequently. The article does, however, contain an important passage on Zululand's place in what he described as the 'world system'. This demonstrates the impact on him at that time of Marxist thought in relation to the global impact of capitalism:

> Since Zululand is a territorial section of the world system, its developments are determined by structural relationships in the whole system. Relations between national and racial groups, between capitalist employers and their employees, between skilled and unskilled labourers, between trade unionists and non-trade unionists, between peasants and industrialized proletariat, which are common to the world system despite great cultural, and indeed structural diversity, therefore produce similar movements in all parts of the system. These movements, with subsidiary variations, occur in Europe, China, Malaya, America, Zululand, etc. In each they take very similar as well as very different cultural forms. In Zululand these are expressed in terms of many cultures: of world culture, as trade unionism, anti-semitism, co-operatives; of native Africa, as labour migration and Ethiopian churches; of South Africa, as ascription by the Zulu of more negrophilism to English than to Boers; and of Zulu culture, as a revival of Zulu ritual. (Gluckman 1958: 62)

The essential points that Gluckman was making were that cultures may differ, but they also interact and overlap. The processes of cultural and social change are, under capitalist influence, the same everywhere. Cultures could no longer be studied in isolation from each other. In demonstrating the place of Zululand in the wider South African and world systems, he came close to the position later suggested by Edmund Leach and by Elizabeth Colson that no boundaries could be drawn around societies, though he continued to be interested in the functioning of systems.

The issue of cultural similarity and difference remained fundamental to Gluckman's work for the rest of his life. While he never denied that there were differences between cultures, he felt the political need to assert that the similarities were greater than the differences and that, in any case, the processes by which cultures functioned and changed were universal. In a sense, this was the underlying theme of the whole of Gluckman's later work on Lozi jurisprudence, of his book *The Judicial Process among the Barotse*, in which 'traditional' court cases were indexed as in a standard legal text, and of his well-known article 'The Reasonable Man in Barotse Law', which emphasized the universality of legal norms.[4] This was the basic issue at the root in the argument in which Gluckman became involved in the last years of his life with Leach and Rodney Needham, who had suggested that he underestimated the significance of cultural differences. In his posthumously published article 'Anthropology and Apartheid: The Work of South African Anthropologists', Gluckman observed that cultures remained different in some respects and alike in others, but it was the fact of similarity that 'the protagonists of apartheid, political and scholarly, are finding most obstinate'. He pointed out that:

> It is possible in the cloistered seclusion of King's College, Cambridge (or Merton College, Oxford) [Edmund Leach (1910–89) was then Provost of King's College and Rodney Needham (1923–2006) was a fellow of Merton College] to put the emphasis on the obstinate differences: it was not possible for 'liberal' South Africans confronted with the policy of segregation within a nation into which the others had been brought, and treated as different – and inferior. (Gluckman 1975: 29)

THE SIGNIFICANCE OF THE 'ANALYSIS'

There can be little doubt that the first of the three articles in the 'Analysis', often referred to by followers of the 'Manchester School' as 'the Bridge', was the most influential of Gluckman's many publications. It is a little surprising that Robert Gordon can only find a 'measly' (his word) forty-eight references to the 'Analysis' in the Library of Science Citation Index – he finds five times as many citations for a 1963 essay 'Gossip and Scandal' (Gordon 2018: 152). A search by this author of Google Scholar in July 2022 found no less than 1,412 citations for the *Bantu Studies* (1940) publication of the 'Analysis' – the largest number for any of Gluckman's articles – and that does not include references to the more frequently cited 1958 reprint of the three articles by the Rhodes-Livingstone Institute.[5] Gluckman's most frequently cited book is *Custom and Conflict in Africa* (1956), a collection of six broadcast talks given on the BBC Third Programme in 1955, with 2,398 Google Scholar citations. This book includes a rewriting of the themes of the 'Analysis' as 'The Bonds in the Colour Bar'. It is undoubtedly through this broadcast, and its subsequent publication in the book, that the themes of the 'Analysis' relating to social change in Zululand have reached the widest audience. It is probably true that the relative inaccessibility of the *Bantu Studies* articles meant that the impact of the 'Analysis', beyond Gluckman's immediate intellectual circle, was somewhat delayed – at least until after the 1958 publication.

The 'Analysis' has to be understood in the context of the prevailing practice of British social anthropologists, under the influence of Malinowski and Radcliffe-Brown, in the 1930s. There were, of course, exceptions and there was increasing awareness of 'social change', but their typical products were studies of individual 'tribes' written in the 'ethnographic present'. They tended to combine evidence from literary sources, the recollections of old men and contemporary fieldwork observations, and to describe a mythical present in which all references to the impact of colonial rule, labour migration, land alienation and modern technology were omitted. Even photographs were carefully selected so as not to reveal the telltale signs of 'culture contact' and pollution. Members of the chosen societies were described as behaving in the ethnographic present in ways in which they were certainly no longer behaving in the real present.[5]

While the 'Analysis' contains explicit attacks on Malinowski's view of history and the social field, including the concept of 'culture contact', which were to be greatly expanded and elaborated in his later publication *Malinowski's Sociological Theories* (1949), it is as remarkable for its implicit and unstated critique of contemporary social anthropological practice. This lies almost as much in its shape and its form as in its substance. The description and analysis of events in real time – the actual present – implied a rejection of the ethnographic present and of hypothetical or conjectural reconstructions, and an acceptance of the need to study all societies in the context of the modern world. Radcliffe-Brown believed that there was no room for named individuals – 'Tom, Dick and Harry' – in the published work of social anthropologists, which should consist of conclusions abstracted from real situations.

In presenting raw data from his notebooks, and describing real people in real situations, as well as his own role and the way in which his presence may have influenced events, Gluckman was not only breaking this rule, but was also reversing the usual procedure, which did allow for the presentation of 'apt illustrations' of previously stated principles. Gluckman's adoption of this style of presentation was primarily related to the definition of the social field. The point of identifying the actors at the bridge, and at the later meetings, was to emphasize the fundamental theme that Zulu and whites in Zululand, and Blacks and Whites in South Africa as a whole, 'form together a single community with specific modes of behaviour to one another' (Gluckman 1958: 9) Only by insisting on this point, he argued, was it possible to understand the behaviour of the people as he had described it.

There is no need to labour the point that the 'Analysis' constitutes a systematic assault on the concept of the 'bounded tribe'. When comparing 'heterogeneous' and 'homogeneous' culture groups, Gluckman came to doubt the existence of homogeneous groups and to suggest that all societies consist of heterogeneous groups insofar as there are always culture variations relating to age and political status (Gluckman 1958: 55). The 'Analysis' is, however, much more than a refutation of the notion of the 'bounded tribe'. After describing the formation of the Zulu Nation from a congeries of small 'tribes', he analysed the development of the

'Zulu-White community' as a result of the intersection of the Zulu and European social systems and the creation of 'a new field of relationships between Blacks and Whites which engendered new forms of conflict and co-operation' (35).

There were both liberal integrationist and Marxist elements in Gluckman's perception of the Zulu-White and Black-White communities of Zululand and South Africa as divided along racial lines by what he described as 'the developing dominant cleavage'. In presenting his material, he was driven, as has already been suggested, by the need not only to demonstrate the impossibility of segregation, but also to distance South African social anthropology from segregation.

Paul Cocks (2001) has made a strong case for the 'Analysis' as a response to W.M. Macmillan's critique of social anthropology, as he had expressed it in *Complex South Africa* (1930) and *Africa Emergent* (1938). In both books he had suggested that anthropology, with its emphasis on separate, bounded and different cultures, and its neglect of history, had provided intellectual support for segregationist politicians. Referring in *Complex South Africa* to 'the new fashion of anthropological studies, for which in the government of native races excessive claims are sometimes made', he had suggested that while:

it is true that the utter want of knowledge and understanding of the native mind and language has caused untold ills, disintegration has already gone too far in the Union of South Africa to admit of any simple refurbishing of the apparatus of tribal organization and custom. Undue stress on the different mentality of the Bantu too often becomes the excuse for shutting the eyes to the unpleasant [an ironic adjective] fact that the Bantu are ordinary human beings, and that the bulk of them are inextricably entangled in and dependent on our own economic system.

He had concluded that: 'By our own act the blacks are part of us and segregation is impossible' (Macmillan 1930: 8, 279, quoted in Cocks 2001: 729–56).

In *Africa Emergent*, Macmillan had included a longer critique of social anthropology, concluding that: 'The short truth is that the scientist [anthropologist], though shy of politics and inclined to mark out a distinct sphere of "primitive" economics, arrives by a different road at a like conclusion to that of the segregationist politician' (1938: 376–77).

There can be little doubt that in writing the 'Analysis', Gluckman was responding to Macmillan and making a social anthropological case for the impossibility of segregation and for seeing South Africa as a single society. When he rewrote the 'Analysis' for the BBC and *Custom and Conflict* in 1955–56, sixteen years later, he added a postscript that linked the 'Analysis' and his updated essay, 'The Bonds in the Colour Bar', to apartheid:

> I myself saw – and enjoyed – many friendly relationships between Whites and Blacks during the first years of my life, and while I was doing research in the field. But as the policy of *apartheid* is applied more and more consistently, any sort of amicable or loyal relations between Whites and Blacks become impossible. Those sections within the White group which were linked in some friendly relationship with sections of the Black group, are being attacked. This is symbolic of deepening, irresoluble, unbalanced, conflict. If these sorts of links are eliminated, Black will deal with White only as authoritarian ruler and employer, always as an enemy, and never as an ally. (Gluckman 1956: 164–65)

In writing the 'Analysis' in 1939, Gluckman was writing primarily as a 'liberal integrationist', but his new acquaintance with Marxism meant that he was also interested in the possibility of revolutionary change in South Africa and sought to explain why it did not happen. In looking back into Zulu history, he identified periods of relative stability of 'repetitive equilibria' when change could be contained within the system, and of changing equilibrium when change could not be contained and led to a radical transformation of the system.

The 1930s were, in Gluckman's view, a time of changing equilibrium. The 'developing dominant cleavage' must eventually lead to a radical transformation and a new system, but it was improbable that this radical change would occur in the short term. In seeking to explain this paradox of cleavage, opposition and relative stability, Gluckman drew on a number of sources: the Marxist theory of contradiction, the Freudian notion of ambivalence, Gregory Bateson's idea of 'schismogenesis', the work of Evans-Pritchard on 'situational selection' and that of Fortes on 'fission and fusion' (Gluckman 1958: 26, fn. 2).

Ronnie Frankenberg has made a strong case for the influence of literary modernism on what he prefers to call 'the Bridge'. He sees it as beginning 'the transformation of the scope of social anthropology beyond the internal or external colonial order toward more sophisticated theoretical possibilities in the same way as did similar developments in literature ([James] Joyce's *Ulysses*, [and Virginia] Woolf's *Mrs Dalloway* . . . for example' (Frankenberg 2005: 178). Given Gluckman's wide reading, it is not too farfetched to see some influence from *Ulysses* and a parallel between a day in the life of Leopold Bloom in Dublin (16 June 1904) and a day in the life of Max Gluckman in Zululand (7 January 1938).

Gluckman saw his analysis of the event at the bridge as a 'cross-section' study in which he examined the interaction of individuals and groups at a shared moment of celebration. He was, in reality, asking himself and seeking to explain how it was that a joint celebration of this kind was possible at all. Why did the participants who represented such violently opposed groups and interests not come to blows? Fundamental to his answer to this question was that in all social relations there are elements of both fission and fusion. For all the pressures driving Blacks and whites apart along the lines of race and caste, there were compensating pressures that made for the cooperation of individuals and groups. A variety of factors made for cohesion and at least temporary stability. One factor was the community of interests created by membership, however unequal, of a single economic system.

The 'Analysis' has been recognized as a pioneering attempt to introduce capitalism, colonialism and conflict into 'structural-functionalist' discourse, but it has also been criticized by some Marxists, such as Maurice Bloch in *Marxism and Anthropology*, for its failure to break out of a Durkheimian (and Radcliffe-Brownean) preoccupation with social cohesion, and for not being Marxist enough. Bloch acknowledged that 'some of Gluckman's theoretical assumptions seem to have been influenced by Marxist ideas', but he thought that 'he never adopted an overall theory that could usefully be described as Marxist'. Frankenberg thought that he had never really undertaken a systematic study of Marxism in the way that Raymond Firth, Peter Worsley, Victor Turner, or he himself had done (Bloch 1983: 143–44; Frankenberg 2005: 175).

Jack Simons, a leading member of the Communist Party of South Africa until its banning in 1950, thought that Gluckman had in the 'Analysis' portrayed 'the white man as a bridge between Zulu tribesmen'. He thought that he was overly impressed by Braadvedt, 'an authority on Zulu history and traditions, but an official of a regime committed to keeping the tribes in a state of subordination'. He suggested, perhaps unfairly, that Gluckman had 'isolated the bridge episode from its setting of colonial conquest and that was a serious theoretical and historical error, the more so because he was a Marxist, probably a [communist] party member at that time' (Macmillan papers: Jack Simons to Hugh Macmillan, 21 July 1993). Simons had also written that Gluckman's portrayal of the Native Commissioner as 'not only an agent of repression, but also a social worker, a political advisor to rural communities and a bridge between settlers and Africans' meant that he was better suited to cooperation with the colonial administration, as Director of the Rhodes-Livingstone Institute, than his less obviously radical predecessor Godfrey Wilson (Simons 1977: 263).

Marvin Harris, an unorthodox Marxist, felt that Gluckman's attack on Malinowski for failing to deal with conflict was a case of a man in a glass house throwing stones, because he had himself failed to deal adequately with the problem (Harris 1968:

554–60). More positively, when reviewing the 1958 edition of the 'Analysis', Lloyd Fallers, author of *Bantu Bureaucracy* and other works, described it as 'the most successful application thus far of the Marxian perspective to anthropological materials and also, perhaps, our single most important study of social change in Africa'. Fallers also said that he was embarrassed to find how much he had made 'the ideas his own without remembering and acknowledging the source' (Fallers 1959: 1122).

DELAYED IMPACT ON
SOUTH AFRICAN AND ZULU STUDIES

In his introduction to the 1958 edition of the 'Analysis', J.C. Mitchell noted that it was 'sad to record [that] in spite of the increasing importance of race relations in South Africa (or possibly because of it), there appear to have been no further studies of this sort, based as they are on intensive field-work methods. They still remain the best on the subject of social change among an important Bantu people in South Africa' (Gluckman 1958: vii–viii). It is indeed a curious fact that the 'Analysis' had, as a radical and Marxist-influenced study, neither immediate successors nor imitators within South African social anthropology. It would be difficult to find any social scientific writing on South Africa from 1942 to 1970 that was as radical in its critique of South African society. Unlike many later studies, it showed an explicit awareness, for instance, of the effects of land alienation and land shortage, and showed up the self-serving absurdity of the commonly held white view that the Zulu were interested in the quantity, not the quality, of their cattle. Gluckman also pointed to the 'pseudo-genetics, pseudo-sociology, pseudo-psychology, pseudo-history etc.' with which South Africa's whites justified their privileges (Gluckman 1958: 63, 67).

In the context of the Cold War, it was almost certainly the fear of accusations of communism, to which Gluckman had earlier been subjected, that inhibited the pursuit of many of his themes in the next thirty years.[6] Philip and Iona Mayer's work on East

London, *Townsmen or Tribesmen* (1961), was greatly influenced
by Gluckman's work, but eschewed political comment or criticism. Absolom Vilakazi's book *Zulu Transformations* (1965)
made no reference to Gluckman at all. D.H. Reader's *Zulu Tribe
in Transition* (1966) acknowledged his help and made a score of
references to his work, but only one was to the 'Analysis'.

It was perhaps only later, with the new interest in 'the invention of tradition' and 'traditionalism', which Gluckman had anticipated in his treatment of the revival of support for the Zulu King,
that the significance of the 'Analysis' came to be fully recognized
in South Africa. In introducing *The Ambiguities of Dependence
in South Africa: Class, Nationalism and the State in Twentieth-
Century Natal*, Shula Marks noted that her book focused on
'events', beginning with the meeting at Eshowe in 1930 between
Solomon ka Dinuzulu and the Governor-General, Lord Athlone.
She thought that in dealing with Zululand-Natal, she 'was sub-
consciously influenced by Max Gluckman's classic *Analysis of a
Social Situation in Modern Zululand*, based on field research completed in 1937 [actually 1938]' only a few years after the episode
she describes: 'There seem to be echoes in Solomon's encounter
with the Earl of Athlone in Gluckman's brilliant and famous description of the opening of the bridge in Zululand in 1938.' She
hoped that she had moved beyond its functionalism even if she
could not 'vie with the intimate detail of his field research and the
vividness of his eye-witness account' (Marks 1986: 9).

Gluckman continued to work on Zulu anthropology and history for the rest of his life, but he never published the promised
book on the subject. He was at first reluctant to give permission
for the 1958 reprint of the 'Analysis' because, as he told Mitchell, his ideas on social change had matured in the previous fifteen years and he would possibly 'rephrase the problems today'.
Mitchell noted:

> We felt, however, that when he eventually publishes his full
> analysis of Zululand as he knew it in the middle thirties, it
> will be a different sort of analysis from the one presented
> here. He will approach the problems again after many

years of comparative reading, of experience of other societies, and of reflection. His analysis will be correspond-
ingly more complete and penetrating, but in the meantime,
these early essays, written when their author had only recently returned from the field and the problems were vivid
in his mind, will always possess a freshness and a vitality
which makes them particularly useful as teaching material.
(Gluckman 1958: viii)

Gluckman told Mitchell that the manuscript of the book in which
the essays would have been incorporated was burnt, together
with many of his Lozi fieldwork notes, in a fire at his camp in
Barotseland in 1940. He told Jack Simons in November 1946 that
he was 'still plodding on with the book on the Zulu' (Emmanuel
College: Gluckman to Simons, 8 November 1946).[7] It is possible that he was then referring to the manuscript of *Conflict and
Cohesion in Zululand*, which survives in the Gluckman papers at
the Royal Anthropological Institute. Part of this manuscript was
published by Robert Gordon in 2014 (Gluckman 2014).

Gluckman was still working on a substantial manuscript, *The
Rise of the Zulu Nation*, at the time of his death, and it was described as 'in the press', but it was never published. A 200-page
manuscript survives.[8] The first half deals with the rise of small
Nguni states from 1500 to 1800 and the second half covers the
rise of Shaka and the Zulu kingdom. A highly condensed and
well-illustrated article on these themes was published in *Scientific
American* in 1960 under the title of 'The Rise of a Zulu Empire'.
The most controversial aspect of the article, and of the manuscript on which it was based, is Gluckman's application of his
knowledge of Freudian psychoanalysis, acquired as an analysand
since the writing of the 'Analysis', to King Shaka's relationship
with his mother, Nandi, and to women in general. He concluded
that Shaka 'was at least a latent homosexual and possibly psychotic' (Gluckman 1960: 157–69). He published a longer version
of this essay in 1974 (Gluckman 1974: 113–44). He then referred
to the existence of his longer unpublished manuscript, which he
described as 'to some extent inconclusive' (1974: 114). In this ar-

ticle, one of the last that he published in his lifetime, he went into more detail about state formation among the Nguni, King Shaka's military tactics, and his establishment of regiments of celibate warriors. He then described him as a 'near psychotic' who had 'a very disturbed psychosexuality' (1974: 140).

INFLUENCE THROUGH THE RLI
AND THE 'MANCHESTER SCHOOL'

While the 'Analysis' may only have had a delayed impact on South African and Zulu studies, it had a more rapid impact in south-central Africa through Gluckman's personal influence on the Rhodes-Livingstone Institute in Northern Rhodesia and through the emerging 'Manchester School'. In introducing the 1958 edition of the 'Analysis', J.C. Mitchell had said that these essays were likely to rank in the future as 'important milestones' in the development of social anthropological theory:

> It is in these essays that Gluckman first outlined an approach to the study of social change, which he has subsequently developed, and which has provided the central set of analytical concepts of the school of anthropology he is building up in Manchester. (Gluckman 1958: vii–viii)

Mitchell had himself provided an outstanding example of the direct influence of the 'Analysis' in his short monograph, *The Kalela Dance* (1958), a study of the Northern Rhodesian Copperbelt, which begins with the analysis of a single event and uses that as the basis for the study of the entire social context with special emphasis on urban ethnicity.

There are numerous references in the anthropological literature, as in Evens and Handelman's edited collection *The Manchester School* (2006), to the importance of the 'Analysis' as a foundational text for the Rhodes-Livingstone Institute and the 'Manchester School'. In the concluding essay in that collection,

Bruce Kapferer wrote: 'Situational analysis and the extended-case method saw their beginnings in Gluckman's analysis of a bridge opening – in the study of a particular event or case' (Kapferer 2006: 320). As the description of events occurring on a single day, the 'Analysis' may be a case study, but it can hardly be described as an extended case study.[9] Richard Werbner has gone so far as to refer to 'a tendency to canonize' the 'Analysis' and has pointed to some arguments against its foundational significance. Emanuel Marx, for example, has pointed out that the wealth of case material assembled by Gluckman in *The Judicial Process among the Barotse of Northern Rhodesia* (1955) 'probably influenced the development of the Manchester School more than Gluckman's *Analysis*' (Marx, quoted in Werbner 2020: 195).

Writing in November 1965 in the introduction to Epstein's edited collection *The Craft of Social Anthropology* (1967), Gluckman himself sought to place the 'Analysis' in the context of successive anthropological generations, and of his own work:

My younger colleagues tell me that they see in my *Analysis of a Social Situation in Modern Zululand* (1940) some of the beginnings of the developments I have been outlining . . . One of them has told me that I was there on the way to making the kind of analysis of how the many different components in a social system operate with varying weight in different kinds of situations. He asked why I had not followed up this kind of analysis and said it would be interesting for students if I recorded the reason. Perhaps this was because it was ahead of its time, and I belonged after all to my own generation. In my own autobiographical recollection, I know that I went to modern Zululand after working for years in the library on their indigenous culture. Bored with this, I plunged with zest into an investigation of their modern life. Had I returned to Zululand, I almost certainly would have gone further in that direction. Instead, the chances of life took me to Barotseland, where I became fascinated by their complex, and not properly recorded,

traditional political system; and then in the problems of
their judicial process and jurisprudential ideas – all legiti-
mate fields of study. But I can salute here the advances the
new generation is making, and feel pleased that I may have
helped them on their way. (Epstein 1967: xix–xx)

NOTES

1. *Analysis of a Social Situation in Modern Zululand* was published as a pamphlet, with a foreword by J.C. Mitchell, by Manchester University Press
   on behalf of the Rhodes-Livingstone Institute in 1958. It consists of three
   articles, which were originally published in Johannesburg as 'Analysis of
   a Social Situation in Modern Zululand: (A) The Social Organization of
   Modern Zululand' and '(B) Social Change in the History of Zululand',
   Bantu Studies, 14 (1940), 1–30 and 147–74, and 'Some Processes of Social Change from Zululand', *African Studies*, 1 (1942), 243–60. As it is
   more accessible, all references here are to the 1958 publication.
2. Gluckman emphasized that the term 'race' was used unscientifically in
   South Africa. He was using it to 'indicate the basis of social groupings,
   not the scientific demarcation of races'.
3. He developed the idea of repetitive systems in his 1953 Frazer Lecture
   Rituals of Rebellion in South-East Africa (1954), in which he examined
   rituals of rebellion associated with the Zulu goddess, Nomkubulwana,
   and, drawing on the work of Hilda Kuper, the Swazi first-fruits ceremony
   and ritual of kingship, the *Ncwala*.
4. These texts will be discussed in a later chapter.
5. This section on the 'Analysis' follows closely my 'Return to the Malungwana Drift' (Macmillan 1995: 39–65).
6. This may not have been only a South African phenomenon. According
   to Maurice Bloch, 'the desperate search for academic respectability by
   British anthropologists in the period 1920–60 ensured that on the whole
   they kept well away from dangerous political associations' (Bloch 1983:
   142).
7. These papers were consulted by the author at Emmanuel College Cambridge, circa 1994, but they are no longer there.
8. Copy in author's possession courtesy of Ivan Karp.
9. Gluckman himself thought that the extended case study began with J.C.
   Mitchell's *The Yao Village* (1956) and was developed by Victor Turner in
   Schism and Continuity in an African Society (1957) (Gluckman 1973b).

CHAPTER 3

MAX GLUCKMAN AT THE RHODES-LIVINGSTONE INSTITUTE IN NORTHERN RHODESIA, 1939–47

• • •

Gluckman had written the first two articles in the 'Analysis' trilogy while staying with Godfrey Wilson in Livingstone during a period of great uncertainty. Although he was appointed on 1 October 1939, his position in the Rhodes-Livingstone Institute was only confirmed in December. If the outbreak of world war, and Max's attitude to it, had precipitated one crisis, there were to be two more crises, which threatened his position and gave him a reputation as accident-prone. It had always been understood that he would do his fieldwork in Barotseland, the Lozi kingdom, Bulozi, which was a protectorate, covering about 45,000 square miles, with a population of about 250,000, within the larger protectorate of Northern Rhodesia. The usual way to get to its administrative capital, Mongu, which was close to Lealui, the royal capital of the *Litunga*, paramount chief or king, Yeta III, was by a 300-mile journey up the Zambesi River by barge. Max and Mary Gluckman set off for Mongu on R.F. Sutherland's barge in mid-December, but they were soon compelled to return to Livingstone after Max accidentally shot and killed the barge *induna* or foreman. He had apparently stood up as Max was shooting at a bird. After a formal inquest by the district commissioner at

Sesheke, the district in which the accident took place, Max was charged with manslaughter and summoned to appear in the high court in Livingstone. The charges were eventually dropped and he paid £35 (about £2,000 in 2023) in compensation to the family of Sandala the *induna*. Mary Gluckman was shocked by these events and was reluctant to set off again, but she was eventually persuaded to do so. They set off once more with Max's research assistant, Davidson Silumesi Sianga, in late January 1940, arriving in Mongu on 17 February (Brown 1979: 529–30; Morrow 2016: 168–69; Gordon 2018: 201–4).

The Gluckmans established a camp at Katongo, about six miles south of Mongu on the road to Sefula, the headquarters of the old-established Paris Evangelical Mission, a French Protestant church, and began fieldwork and learning the siLozi language. They did not have a car, but they did have horses, which were a useful mode of transport. Their camp was about fifteen miles from Lealui, the royal capital, which was in the centre of the plain, and rather further from Limulunga, the dry season capital to which the *Litunga* and his court migrated annually by royal barge in the picturesque *Kuomboka* ceremony. The Gluckmans must have spent a good deal of time at Lealui and Limulunga, as attendance at the *kuta* and the recording of court cases became an important part of Max's work. It would have been difficult for them to commute daily from Katongo to either place, so they may also have camped there. Over time, they seem to have established a small village at Katongo with Lozi-style homes not only for themselves, but also for several research assistants, and for domestic staff, some of whom they brought with them from Livingstone. They soon seemed to be well settled and were beginning to learn the language and establish a relationship with the local people.

Their position there was not, however, entirely secure. Katongo may have seemed to be remote from the war, but within less than six months of their arrival, Max was in trouble again – this time it was on account of his allegedly subversive, or anti-war, views, which appear to have been reported by a junior district officer. Members of the provincial administration – colonial civil servants – were notoriously suspicious of anthropologists and were apparently alarmed by Gluckman's practice of discussing the war with members of the *kuta*, or Barotse national council, at Lealui. This crisis blew up in July and Max had to fly in a small plane from Mongu to Lusaka early in August for an urgent interview with the governor, Sir John Maybin. He persuaded the governor of his loyalty, but it was agreed that he should be given three months' notice after which he would leave to join the army. Godfrey Wilson, who must have known that his own position in Northern Rhodesia was insecure, persuaded the governor that this period should be extended to enable Max to complete at least one piece of published research based on his fieldwork. This was fortuitous because Godfrey Wilson, who was a pacifist and conscientious objector, and had his own problems with the war, submitted his resignation as director of the institute in November and left in March 1941. The last straw had been his exclusion by the Broken Hill mining company from its compound – his fieldwork area. Its managers were worried by his familiarity with its African workers and his habit of smoking with them. Monica Wilson, his widow, said later that he had resigned because 'he was not prepared to carry out urban research from an office' (Wilson 1977: 283).

Godfrey Wilson had submitted a confidential report to the governor in defence of Gluckman on 18 July. Allowing himself to undertake some amateur psychoanalysis, he attributed Gluckman's 'adolescent arrogance and aggressiveness' to the effects of the antisemitism that he had encountered in South Africa. He argued that:

> His political views are largely a pose and I know him to be passionately desirous of an Allied victory. He also, if I may give a parallel, has satirical views on love; but he is, in fact, happily married and devoted to his wife. In so far as his political views are serious they arise from a deep dissatisfaction with the endemic warfare and unemployment and the inefficient boom-slump rhythm of our social system, and a belief that these things are avoidable . . .

If Your Excellency feels able to send him back to Barotseland I am certain that the shock of the incident will finally
bring to the surface the underlying integrity and responsibility which his friends, and I myself, recognize in him.

The loss to the Institute and to Social Anthropology which
his professional ruin would bring would be considerable.
His reputation already stands high, and I am not alone in
thinking him capable of great things; several eminent anthropologists have told me that they have learnt much from
discussion with him. Were his career now to be checked
my share of the responsibility would weigh heavily on me;
I should feel that I had failed to convey to the Board his real
qualities. Nor could we replace him, for potentially first-
class anthropologists are few. (Brown 1979: 529–30)

The Gluckmans were based together at Katongo for most of 1940
and returned to Livingstone in December. Max became acting
director of the institute in April 1941 and returned to Katongo
for a further ten months fieldwork in January 1942. Mary then
went to Johannesburg to await the birth of their first child, John,
who was born there in March. She cannot have returned to Barotseland before the middle of the year and then stayed in Mongu.
Max was the only anthropologist on the staff of the institute from
April 1941 until the arrival of three postwar recruits in 1946.
While in Barotseland in 1942, he had to run the institute by remote control. It was initially anticipated that Audrey Richards
(1899–1984), who had been head of the Social Anthropology
Department at the University of Witwatersrand, would take over
as director, but she decided not to do so, preferring to remain in
London where she was working in the Colonial Office as a wartime civil servant and was involved in setting up the Colonial Social Science Research Council. Gluckman was not confirmed as
substantive director of the institute until 1943 – he then held the
position until 1947 (Wilson 1977: 279–83).

In their first year in Barotseland – now better known as Bulozi – Max and Mary Gluckman worked with Davidson Silumesi

Figure 3.1. Max and Mary Gluckman with a carved walking stick, Barotseland, probably Mongu, 1940. © RAI. 400.052726

Sianga and Prince Mwendaweli(e)[1] Lewanika – a son of King Lewanika I and half-brother of four *Litungas*: Yeta III, Imwiko I, Mwanawina III and Lewanika II – as research assistants. They were both trained by Gluckman in research methods, including court-case recording and diary-keeping, and continued to work in his absence. Sianga remained on the institute's staff until 1955 and Lewanika, who was later *mulena* or prince at Naliele and then at Mwandi, remained until 1949. As a team they gathered a great deal of material on the complex ecology of the central Barotse plain, which lies on the upper Zambesi River. It extends for 125 miles from north to south and twenty-five miles from east to west – and is the heart of Bulozi. They also gathered information on the political system, as well as genealogies, village censuses and information on household income. This demographic data was intended to shed light on the impact of labour migration on Bulozi – a matter of great concern to the administration. In another of the accidents to which the Gluckmans were prone at this time, a fire destroyed their homestead at Katongo when they were away from home in September 1940. This not only destroyed the draft manuscript of a book on the Zulu and some related material, but also most of eight months' collection of ethnographic and gene-

Figure 3.2. Max Gluckman at work, Barotseland, 1940. © RAI. 400 .032406

alogical data. The ecological and political data survived because Max had carried it with him. This may have influenced the shape and content of his first published work on Barotseland – *Economy of the Central Barotse Plain* (Gluckman 1968a: ix).

ECONOMY OF THE CENTRAL BAROTSE PLAIN

This monograph, which was written up in Livingstone in 1941, sounds and reads a little like a Marxist study of the material base. It seems, however, to have been inspired rather less by Marx than by Evans-Pritchard's then new book *The Nuer* (1940), a study of a similarly transhumant people, and by C.G. Trapnell and J. Clothier's *The Soils, Vegetation and Agricultural Systems of North-Western Rhodesia* (1937), a pioneering work of ecology (spelt 'oecology' by Gluckman). The latter book covers Barotseland in great detail, and Gluckman consulted Trapnell while writing his monograph.

Figure 3.3. Mary Gluckman at work, Barotseland, 1940. © RAI. 400.031564

Economy of the Central Barotse Plain includes frequent comparisons with Zululand. Gluckman points, for example, to the relative lack of importance of cattle in the Lozi economy and to the relatively greater importance of farming, fishing and local trade. This monograph does not, however, have a great deal in common with the 'Analysis'. Although it looks at Barotseland at two dates – precolonial, circa 1880, and colonial, since 1900 – it lacks the historical content and emphasis of the 'Analysis'. It makes no reference to 'events', equilibria or repetitive and changing systems. Gluckman refers to the books of early travellers, such as David Livingstone, and to those of more recent French missionaries, some of which Mary translated, but he had no access to archival sources.

With its multiplicity of twenty-five 'tribes' or 'ethnic groups' – the latter was not a category that Gluckman ever used until a much later date – and its complex system of seasonal transhu-

Figure 3.4. Gluckman's photo of Silumesi Davidson Sianga, his long-serving research assistant, Barotseland, 1940. © RAI. 400.0303532

mance between mounds on the flood plain and the plain margins and 'Bush', Bulozi was, of course, very different from Zululand. The greatest similarity between the two studies comes in the concluding chapter where Gluckman looks at the place of Barotseland in the world economy, and at the increasing importance of money, international trade and labour migration. He states:

Whites and Lozi are now members of a single economic system in which there is a large field of White-Lozi relationships which affect all relationships within Lozi social organisation . . . Briefly, most Lozi have become peasant-wage labourers in the world economy. Whites on the whole are dominant: they are administrators, employers, and skilled workers, traders, with a higher standard of living than the Lozi. However, we have seen that a certain number of influ-

ential Lozi, like the paramount chief, are able themselves to
become employers of Lozi labour. (Gluckman 1968a: 119)

In the only direct reference to the 'Analysis', Gluckman noted that
'[t]o me coming from Zululand, the absence of conflict in White-
Lozi relations was remarkable'. He thought that in Barotseland, as
opposed to some other parts of Northern Rhodesia, this might be
due to the treaty rights enjoyed by the Lozi monarchy and to the
fact that the whites had not taken land. The people were able to
subsist on their own land and were not dependent on money for
their daily needs as they were in the labour centres, such as the
Copperbelt, where there was more conflict, as had been demonstrated by strikes in 1935 and 1940 (Gluckman 1968a 119, 121).
    In a further comparison Gluckman noted:

> In Zululand and Natal where the Africans have lost much
> land and live under harsher social conditions, the economic
> struggle against the Whites is re-uniting the shattered Zulu
> nation and bringing in even tribes which were never part of
> it; in Barotseland, the tribes do not feel the same economic
> pressure, and under the protection of the British Govern-
> ment the Lubale [Luvale] and Lunda have got their inde-
> pendence [from Lozi control]. (1968a: 121–22)

Gluckman's first period in Barotseland coincided with good rains
and a good flood on the Zambesi. He shared Livingstone's view
of the kingdom as he had seen it in 1853 as 'a land flowing with
milk and honey'. He quoted Trapnell and Clothier's 1937 report
on the relative impoverishment of the area after the outbreak of
bovine pleuro-pneumonia and the end of cattle exports in 1915,
and the Pim-Milligan report of 1938 on the rise of labour migration, and the absence of 50–60% of men from the Mongu and
Sesheke districts, but he did not emphasize impoverishment.
He noted changes like the permanent migration of some people
from the plain to the margins and the inward migration of the
so-called Wiko (mainly Luchazi, Luvale and Chokwe) who came
as refugees from Portuguese Angola and settled on the western

Bush. There was also some permanent emigration of men, with or without families, to the urban areas of the region. He noted that the shift of economic activity from the mounds in the plain to the margins was reducing the influence of mound-owners, and there was an increasing distance between rulers and people, with the emergence of a Lozi bureaucracy of salaried titleholders. The tone of the monograph seemed, however, to be neutral in relation to the direction of social change.

'BAROTSELAND: WHERE WESTERN CIVILIZATION HAS BROUGHT POVERTY'

After Gluckman's second ten-month period of fieldwork in Bulozi in 1942, when there was a less favourable flood, he took a gloomier view. In 1945 he drafted an article for *Libertas*, a liberal journal in South Africa, entitled 'Barotseland: Where Western Civilization Has Brought Poverty' (manuscript in the author's possession). It was published under the blander title 'Zambesi River Kingdom', with some of Max's own excellent photographs – he was a first-class photographer and took thousands of photos in Barotseland. The article, which is loosely based on *Economy of the Central Barotse Plain*, begins with a reference to G.F. Clay's recently published and official *Memorandum on Post War Planning in Northern Rhodesia* (Clay 1945). In what has been seen as an anticipation of later theories of 'the development of underdevelopment', he noted that:

> The problems to be solved appear in the economic history of Barotseland. The coming of Europeans did not increase the wealth of the people. Its distance from markets and consuming centres has steadily reduced it to comparative poverty, so that in its history we can see the fate of most of Northern Rhodesia. Where the richest part has become poor, the vast regions on poor sandy soils in the north-east are now described [by Audrey Richards] as 'hungry manless areas' . . . for all the men who can leave to work in the mining areas. (Gluckman 1945a: 21)

Gluckman continued with a long quotation from Livingstone's 'milk and honey' description of the area as it was in the 1850s. He elaborated this with his own idyllic description of Bulozi, as it was 'before the coming of the Europeans'. It was then 'the rich heart of a great region, perhaps the richest kingdom in Central Africa'. He offered a utopian description of a precolonial state in which 'all men, from king to commoner, lived on more or less the same standard' and 'subject tribes enjoyed definite advantages in being members of the Lozi kingdom. They participated in the circulation of goods through the tribute system, and they enjoyed the protection of the Paramount in their trading within his boundaries'. He did not suggest that life was perfect: 'tyranny, ignorance and famine were real oppressors, but economic exploitation was absent'. This apparently idyllic state was ended by the introduction of long-distance trade, including the slave trade, and then by the establishment of a British protectorate in 1900 and by increasing inequality. Writing of the contemporary situation, as of 1945, he noted:

> The flood-plain has ceased to be the economic heart of the region. It is still the basis of the Lozis' subsistence, some few of them even make a living there. But Barotseland has become part of the world economy; its people want clothes, pots, sewing-machines, lamps, paraffin, dishes, ever more and more European goods. They have to earn money. From the centres of this new economy, the plain is far distant, and the economic bias has shifted to the Copper Belt. (Gluckman 1945a: 31)

The latter part of the article draws on material that Gluckman collected in Barotseland in 1942 and published in 1943 as *Essays on Lozi Land and Royal Property*. This consisted of two essays: 'Lozi Land Tenure' and 'Property Rights of the Lozi King and Royal Family'. These were Gluckman's first ventures into legal anthropology, which was to be the main focus of his work for the next twenty years. The essay on Lozi land tenure is widely comparative in its scope, taking account of English land and property law, Gluckman's own work on the Zulu, Isaac

Schapera's work on the Tswana, and Audrey Richards's studies of the Bemba, *Hunger and Work in a Savage Tribe* (1932) and *Land, Labour, and Diet in Northern Rhodesia* (1939), and making references to many other societies in and out of Africa. The implications for land ownership of the unusual ecology and transhumant farming system of Barotseland are considered and compared with remarkably different systems, such as *citemene*, or shifting cultivation, among the Bemba in the northern province of Northern Rhodesia. This paper is also significant in providing Gluckman's first tentative presentation of his view of Lozi landholding in terms of a 'hierarchy of estates of holding', from the *Litunga* downwards. He was to develop this view twenty years later in *Ideas in Barotse Jurisprudence* (1965), and it was to be taken up, as we shall see, many years later by social anthropologists writing about Soviet collective farms (Gluckman 1968b: *passim* and 28–29).

COLLECTIVE FARMS

In the section of the essay on 'Lozi Land Tenure', dealing with 'The effects of modern conditions on African land-holding', Gluckman discussed the possibilities for the introduction of co-operative production and collective farming into Southern Africa. After the entry of the USSR into the war in 1941, Soviet and communist references were more acceptable than they may have been previously. 'Lozi Land Tenure' includes an appendix on 'Individual Rights of Ownership in Land and Its Products in the U.S.S.R.'. Drawing mainly on Sidney and Beatrice Webb's *Soviet Communism: A New Civilisation?* (1935), he considered the possibilities for communes, state farms and collective farms in Northern Rhodesia. He noted the persistence of elements of individualism in Lozi agricultural production, and its retention within the Soviet collective farm. He was not the only person to take an interest in the possibilities for collective farms in Southern Africa and he referred to a paper on the topic by Eddie Roux, a South African Marxist and former member of the South African Communist Party, on 'Collective Farming in the Reserves', and to his novel on the theme, *The Cattle of Khumalo*. He also cited a paper by Monica Wilson, who was by no means a communist, on 'Soviet Policy among Primitives'[2] (Gluckman 1968b: 42–3, 61–64 and 69, fn. 100).

There were to be echoes of the Soviet collective farm, though perhaps also of the *kibbutz* or *moshav*, of which Gluckman had firsthand experience in Palestine in 1936, in the 'Proposals to Establish a System of Controlled and Improved Land-Usage among the Tonga'. These were part of the report of the 'reconnaissance survey' on *Land Holding & Land Usage among the Plateau Tonga of Mazabuka District*, of which Gluckman was co-author in 1945. They included proposals for the development of 'social-agricultural' units, with the redistribution of all arable land in a unit into four communal fields with individual strips. There would be a five-year rotation of the communal fields, with three years of maize or millet, one of cowpeas, groundnuts or beans and one year fallow. The system of rotation, known as the Kanchomba system, had been worked out by the agriculture department in previous years. There would also be communal acquisition and use of ploughs and other agricultural machinery, and communal cattle kraals and manuring. Farmers would be encouraged to move into these units with an offer of a higher price for their communally produced maize (Allan et al. 1948: 8–10).

'PROPERTY RIGHTS OF THE LOZI KING'

The essay on the property rights of the king and the royal family starts from the status of the *Litunga* as 'owner of the country' with rights over the allocation of homesteads, something that is compared with the British monarch's claim to be the ultimate owner of all land in his or her kingdom. Gluckman also goes into detail about the king's rights in relation to land, and fisheries, and to the receipt of tribute in labour or goods. He describes the *Litunga*'s receipt of gifts, as opposed to tribute, and his rights in relation to natural products such as ivory, lion skins, hippo skins and rhino horns, and to certain game, such as eland. An appendix quotes, for comparative purposes, the English law relating to the monarch's ownership of all unmarked swans, to a share of all swans on the Thames, as well as to whales and sturgeon.

He describes the process whereby, under the British South Africa Company administration in 1906, serfdom was abolished and unpaid tribute labour was reduced to twelve days a year, in exchange for an annual payment of £850 to the *Litunga* by the administration. Under the new colonial government in 1925, the remaining period of tribute labour, much of which was used for the construction and maintenance of irrigation canals on the central plain, was abolished in exchange for an annual payment to the *Litunga* of £2,500. The *Litunga* could still demand the delivery of goods, such as fishing spears and nets, from the craftsmen who made them, but he now had to pay cash for them.

By 1941, with the entry into the war of the USSR, administrative suspicion of the Gluckmans was reduced and they began to be socially accepted in Livingstone and Mongu. For all that he had a lasting, and probably deserved, reputation for intellectual arrogance, Gluckman was always unfailingly punctilious and generous in his acknowledgement of help. His primary acknowledgement in the *Economy of the Central Barotse Plain* was to Colin Trapnell, who read the essay in proof and made important corrections. As well as Godfrey Wilson and Edward Evans-Pritchard, readers of the manuscript included J. Gordon Read, the provincial commissioner for Barotseland, and at least two other members of the provincial administration. It was also read by three members of the Paris Evangelical Mission, Messieurs A. Jalla, R. Coisson and F. Burger, and by Dr G.M. Childs of the American Mission Board in Angola. Lozi readers included Induna Francis Suu, of Lealui, and Induna Mbasiwana, with the help of Gluckman's research assistant, Davidson Silumesi Sianga (Gluckman 1968a: iv–viii).

Gluckman established a close relationship with Gordon Read, with whom he played chess. Read invited him to write a memorandum on the *Administrative Organization of the Barotse Native Authorities with a Plan for Reforming Them*. This was prompted

by Sir Alan Pim's 1938 report on the financial and economic position of Northern Rhodesia, which commented on the amount
of money that was wasted on payments to the Lozi bureaucracy,
which could be spent more productively (Pim and Milligan
1938). These annual payments were made to Lozi officials as
compensation after the outlawing of tribute payments in 1925.
The situation had been further complicated by the imposition on
Barotseland of Native Authorities and districts as part of the imposition of 'indirect rule' in 1937. This created further confusion
because, as Gluckman pointed out in several places, the Lozi system was based on *makolo*, or sectors, sometimes called by others
'regiments', which included widely scattered people and were
not territorial.

Gluckman provided an extraordinarily detailed account of the
'traditional' Lozi system of government, and its officeholders,
with a plan for reform, which was presented to the provincial
administration in December 1943 for onward transmission to
the Lozi authorities. Somewhat strangely, he indicated that his
proposed changes were contrary to his own principles, as he personally 'favoured a democratic system based on open elections
to the councils of local districts and, for the present, indirect
elections from these to district councils, and thence to a national
council'. He acknowledged that it would be 'useless to advocate
this now'. He did not propose the abolition of any titles as he
thought that this would be unacceptable to the Lozi, but he did
propose ways in which titleholders could be made more useful.
In a letter to 'Paramount Chief Yeta III and the *Ngambela* Wina
in Council' and dated 16 December 1943, he hinted at the need
for modernization:

> I thought it would be a return for all the help you and your
> people have given me in my work, if I explained the history
> of your kutas and the titles of your indunas, and how the po-
> litical organisation came to be what it is . . . With my under-
> standing of your history, as a friend of the Malozi, I advise
> you that the kutas must be brought into line with modern
> needs. To try to keep the past alive only on the past is im-

possible; the past will only remain alive if it draws strength
from the present. (Gluckman 1943: 11 – dated 1943, but
not actually published until July 1944)

Gluckman concluded his letter with the slightly pessimistic comment: 'If you reject my proposals, I hope that my description of
your history and kuta organisation will gain you some understanding from the government.' In the body of his report, he
noted that asking the Lozi to abolish titles would be like asking
the English to abolish hereditary titles such as those of Lord Nel-
son or the Duke of Wellington. His proposals were so detailed
and complicated that it is unlikely that they were fully understood by the provincial administration, let alone the Lozi authorities. He personally lobbied the Governor, Sir John Waddington,
but his proposals had little impact. He revised his memorandum,
following his three-week visit to the Mwandi council, in the
south of Barotseland, in January 1944, and published it in July
1944 as the first of the RLI's mimeographed 'communications'.
It ran to two volumes, including appendices, and to 100 pages
of foolscap. It was typed by Mwendaweli(e) Lewanika and reproduced by Gestetner in Bulawayo, selling for fifteen shillings –
the contemporary price of about a dozen paperbacks. Gluckman
paid a shorter visit to Mwandi in June 1944, which was cut short
by an invitation from Audrey Richards to visit East Africa. In an
introductory note, written after his return, he said that he had
been unable to make further revisions because of the heavy work
involved in planning for the institute's expansion with a Colonial
Development Fund grant – a reference to the application for
funding that is discussed below.

The provincial administration wanted more radical changes
and proceeded in 1946, with the reluctant consent and collabora-
tion of the *Litunga*, with the abolition of old councils and a purge
of traditional titleholders. Gluckman reported that members, at
the first meeting of the 'New Katengo' council, which he may
have attended in 1947, 'attacked their rulers for agreeing, without
consulting them, to the radical changes that had diminished the

glory of their kingship'. Richard Brown, writing in 1979, thought, however, that 'there was some force in their [the administrators'] view that Gluckman had adopted a protective but unprogressive posture in support of an *ancien régime*'. His memorandum was based on material he had collected in 1942 and he acknowledged the help of his research assistants, Davidson Sianga and Mwendaweli(e) Lewanika, and at least eight members of the Lozi royal family, and councillors (Colson and Gluckman 1951: 60–1; Brown 1979: 535–37; Gordon 2018: 247–38).

It was not, however, until 1955, in the introduction to *The Judicial Process among the Barotse*, that Gluckman included a comprehensive acknowledgement of his Lozi helpers. Looking back over a total of twenty-seven months of fieldwork, he thanked the *Litungas* Yeta III and Imwiko, the *Mulena Mukwae* Mulima, princess at Nalolo, and her husband, the *Ishee Kwandu*, the *Ngambelas* (traditional prime ministers), Munalula, Wina and Nalubita, and at least six councillors. Recalling visits in 1940 (ten months), 1942 (ten months) and 1947 (three months), he acknowledged the people of Katongo, his main fieldwork base. He regretted that many of his friends there had passed on, but he named fifteen of the living – 'with their kin, their wives and their children. They were our neighbours and adopted people for many months; we could not ask for better friends'. The people of Katongo had given him the soubriquet 'Makapweka', which he translated as 'generous giver'. He was intensely proud of this nickname and, feeling that it had been purloined by a controversial district commissioner in 1957, he added it beneath his name on the title pages of the reprints of his two Barotse legal books (Gluckman 1973a: xxii–xxv, xxxv).

LATER CRITIQUES OF GLUCKMAN'S LOZI WORK

It has to be said that Gluckman's work on the economy of the central Barotse plain has not stood up well to later scrutiny by academic historians. In *The Hidden Hippopotamus* (1980), Gwyn

Prins was especially critical of Gluckman's fieldwork methods. He translated 'Makapweka' as 'recklessly generous giver', and referring to him, not by name, but as 'one of my predecessors in Bulozi', he suggested, without much specific evidence, that 'he reportedly paid freely for information'. He had consequently 're-ceived a great deal of information from needy and greedy people, cooked for his taste as they understood it' (Prins 1980: 247). Ger-vase Clarence-Smith, in his article on 'Slaves, Commoners and Landlords in Bulozi, 1875–1906', provided a devastating critique, taking issue with Gluckman's portrayal of a precolonial, and egalitarian, Arcadia in Bulozi. He suggested that he had played down the exploitative relations of production which character-ized precolonial Bulozi, including the predominance of a harsh form of slavery, and that he had omitted to mention the evidence for this in David Livingstone's journals. He cited three reasons for Gluckman's failings: an analytical framework that involved 'a quite spurious logical necessity for non-exploitative relations of production'; 'a somewhat cavalier attitude towards historical methods and sources, presenting an almost timeless picture of the pre-colonial past and rejecting written evidence which did not accord with dubious oral traditions'; and 'his anti-colonial sympathies [which] seem to have encouraged him to depict the Lozi past in glowing terms so as to stress the defects of the colo-nial régime' (Clarence-Smith 1979: 219).

Prince Akashambatwa Mbikusita-Lewanika, a prominent Lozi intellectual and politician, a founder of the Movement for Multi-Party Democracy (the MMD) and a son of *Litunga* Lewan-ika II (formerly Godwin Mbikusita-Lewanika), is more apprecia-tive of Gluckman's work. In his important and recent historical work *The Soul of the Barotse People: A Heritage of Land, Labour, Livelihood and Liberty*, he makes frequent references to three of Gluckman's books, and, though believing, mistakenly, that he worked for the Colonial Office, includes him among the inter-national scholars who have written about Barotseland with the benefit of 'their lived experiences' in the kingdom (Mbikusita-Lewanika 2021: 103).

THE MAZABUKA RECONNAISSANCE SURVEY

Gluckman's newfound acceptability in government was confirmed by his receipt of an invitation at the end of 1944 to join
the Native Land Tenure Committee, but he and the government
ecologist Colin Trapnell were almost immediately redirected
early in 1945, after one meeting of the committee, to take part
with William Allan, assistant director of agriculture, and D.U.
Peters, an agricultural officer, in the previously mentioned reconnaissance survey on landholding and land usage among the
plateau Tonga. This urgent wartime survey was prompted by the
belief that there were special problems in the Mazabuka district
of the southern province. These were believed to stem from population pressure, overcultivation, overgrazing and soil erosion, in
an area where there had been considerable alienation of so-called
Crown land to settler farmers along both sides of what is known
in Northern Rhodesia/Zambia as 'the line of rail' – the railway
that links Cape Town to the Congo. The administration was also
alarmed by incipient class formation – the emergence of a group
of Tonga farmers, many of them the products of the Seventh Day
Adventist mission, and a larger group of smallholders, who, it
was alleged, were demanding and obtaining a disproportionate
share of arable land. The reconnaissance mission concluded that
the latter problem was exaggerated. A more serious problem was
the low productivity of the 15,000 subsistence farmers in the
area. This was the problem that the 'social agricultural' units, inspired by the discussion of collective farms outlined above, was
intended to solve (Allan et al. 1948: 1–4, 17–18).

Gluckman was only able to spend four weeks in 1945 doing
fieldwork in Mazabuka district for this project. He chose to carry
out most of his interviews with interpreters who could translate
for him into siLozi and he interviewed some people himself in
siLozi, or in siZulu, which is understood by siNdebele-speakers.
He was, perhaps unnecessarily, apologetic about the inadequacy
of his chapter on social organization, which included detailed
tables, derived from district tax registers, on village size, dis-

tribution and stability. He also pointed to the insecurity in the area caused by land alienation – something that was intensified by the questions asked by members of the Native Land Tenure Committee and by members of the reconnaissance mission itself. He noted that the Tonga feared that these enquiries, and any evidence that they occupied fertile land, might result in a further settler land-grab. The report, which was written up in 1945, and then submitted to the government, was only published in 1948. It then carried a 'comment' on his chapter, written at his request by Elizabeth Colson, a new recruit to the institute, who had done a year's fieldwork among the plateau Tonga in 1946–47. Colson largely confirmed Gluckman's description of Tonga landholding and village organization, with its emphasis on matrilineal succession; the lack of genealogical depth and historical knowledge; and the previous absence of chieftaincy. Chiefs had been arbitrarily chosen and imposed by the colonial government in the 1920s with the establishment of Native Authorities, a feature of indirect rule. Colson did point to elements of patrilineality, which Gluckman may have underestimated, and to the importance of rain shrines (Allan et al 1948: 20–22; and Elizabeth Colson, 'Comment on the Tonga Report' in Allan et al. 1948: 185–92).

Gluckman was the joint author of the whole report with William Allan, and he contributed the chapter on 'Production and Consumption'. This included information from court records on inheritance, from interviews and other sources on labour migration, which was relatively low in the district with 25% male absentees, and important data from sample budgets on household income. This varied from £5 a year for the mass of subsistence farmers to £33 a year for smallholders and £377 a year for the small group of Seventh Day Adventist commercial farmers (Allan et al. 1948: 144–73).

The proposal for 'social agricultural' units, involving radical land redistribution, was presumably the result of discussion by all members of the team, but it is reasonable to assume that the proposals for communal or collective farming were Gluckman's contribution. These ideas, probably spread by the circulation of his essay on 'Lozi Land Tenure', with its appendix on individual land rights in the USSR, do seem to have had an impact among members of the provincial administration, as there were several references to collective farms in the five-year plans that district commissioners were required to write for their districts in 1943.

'SEVEN-YEAR RESEARCH PLAN OF THE RLI'

Gluckman was confirmed as director of the RLI in January 1943 and then spent most of three years – 1943, 1944 and 1945, the last years of the war – living and working in Livingstone. This was the longest time that Max and Mary had spent in Livingstone, a small town, near the Victoria Falls, which had suffered a demotion following the transfer of the capital to Lusaka in 1935. As director of the institute, he had some status in the small town, where a few government departments remained, but he was always glad to get away. He spent two months – February and March 1943 – visiting Lozi migrant labourers on the South African goldmines around Johannesburg. He had been invited to visit by William Gemmill, general manager of the Witwatersrand Native Labour Association (WENELA), the labour recruitment organization. It was on this occasion that he had his last encounter with Godfrey Wilson, who had joined the Army Medical Corps in 1941, serving for six months in North Africa, and had then transferred to the Army Education Scheme, both noncombatant roles. Wilson's impression of Gluckman was, as he told his wife Monica, that he 'had calmed down a lot and become a responsible human being . . . I am so happy about him'. Sadly, Wilson, who had always been prone to depression and should probably not have joined the army in any capacity, took his own life in Johannesburg in May 1944. Gluckman contributed an obituary for Wilson to the first number of the institute journal that he started in June 1944. After meeting him in 1943, he noted that as a result of his time in the army 'his vast store of friendliness and human kindness had been additionally released, and he was quicker at reaching sympathetic understanding with everyone'. In his obituary Gluckman praised Wilson's *Economics of Detribalization*, the results of his work on Broken Hill, which was published in two volumes as Rhodes-Livingstone Papers in 1941 (Gluckman 1944a: 1–3; Morrow 2016: 205, 214).

Gluckman spent two months in 1944 on visits to southern Barotseland, where he did fieldwork. He also visited Kenya and Uganda with Audrey Richards, who was to become the first director of the East African Institute of Social Research at Makerere in Uganda when it was established in 1950. They visited Makerere College, and Gluckman was also pleased to be received in regal style by the ruler of Bunyoro. He was in Livingstone for most of 1945, except for a month in Mazabuka, but he was on secondment there from the institute for the several months that it took him to write up his half of the reconnaissance survey report. He was then absent from Livingstone for most of 1946, spending two months doing fieldwork in what he called Lambaland, rural parts of Ndola district on the Copperbelt, four months in South Africa, training his new recruits, and two months on leave in Britain.

Running the institute, of which he was the only professional employee, should not have been an onerous task, but Gluckman also had a supervisory responsibility for the David Livingstone Memorial Museum (later the Rhodes-Livingstone Museum) in the absence of the substantive curator, the archaeologist Desmond Clark (1916–2002), who had arrived in January 1938, but was absent on military service in East Africa from 1941 to 1946. Clark's wife Betty had acted for him in 1941–42 as curator of the museum and secretary of the institute, but she resigned at the end of the latter year. These posts were separated in 1943, and an acting curator and an acting secretary were appointed, but Gluckman had a continuing responsibility. He took his commitment to the museum seriously, writing several articles on museum-related issues and adding to the museum's collection of *makishi* masks and costumes, and other artefacts. As a result of his initiative and pressure, the institute and the museum were separated in 1946–47.

Gluckman devoted a good deal of energy in 1943–45 to outreach. In addition to extending the series of Rhodes Livingstone Papers, which Godfrey Wilson had started, he inaugurated a series of mimeographed communications in 1944 and a journal, *Human Problems in British Central Africa*, in the same year. He later complained that his launch of the journal was premature and that he had to do a great deal of the writing himself. At the same time, he expanded the reference library, which Mary catalogued, and set up an institute study circle, offering lectures to local residents. People and institutions, both locally and internationally, could become members of the institute and subscribe to its publications. He also began to give broadcasts on the Northern Rhodesian broadcasting service, which was based in the new capital, Lusaka (Gluckman 1948: 64–79).

Among the lectures and broadcast talks that Gluckman gave was one entitled 'The Difficulties, Achievements and Limitations of Social Anthropology', which was also published in the first number of the journal in June 1944. The article was largely addressed to the question whether sociology – he usually preferred to use that term – could ever be a science. He referred to the work of Radcliffe-Brown and Evans-Pritchard. There was a significant number of German Jewish refugees and Lithuanian Jewish traders in Livingstone, and when he introduced into his lecture references to Nazism, antisemitism and 'the new wave of persecutions of Jews', which was later to be known as the Holocaust, he was making points that had a local as well as an international resonance (Gluckman 1944b: 23–45).

Much of Gluckman's energy in 1943–45 was devoted to plans for the future of the institute and to applications for funding, which would be provided in terms of the Commonwealth Development and Welfare Act of 1940, and dispensed by the Colonial Social Science Research Council, which was established in 1944, and in which Audrey Richards played a significant role. Godfrey Wilson had produced draft proposals in 1940, but these had been put to one side when the government decided not to apply for funds during the war. Soon after Gluckman's confirmation as director in January 1943, there was a change of mind and the institute's board of trustees instructed him to draw up new research plans. He had produced a draft plan by September 1943, when it was discussed by the trustees with the governor,

Sir John Waddington (1890–1957), in the chair. Debates about the proposals, and about the relationship between the government and the sociologists, seem to have gone on for some time. Max was prompted to produce a memorandum in April 1944 'on co-operation between government and the Rhodes-Livingstone Institute', in which he argued that administrators should accept criticism without resentment, and quoted in support the USSR, where, he claimed, perhaps surprisingly, that criticism was welcomed in all branches of life.

The plan was submitted for approval by the institute's board of trustees and was still being discussed by provincial commissioners in September 1944. An application for funding to the Colonial Social Science Research Council was approved by the middle of 1944 and a grant of £21,000 to cover three sociologists and an economist for Northern Rhodesia and Nyasaland, for four years, was awarded. Another application was made to the Beit Trust to fund a sociologist for Southern Rhodesia, which did not fall under the Colonial Office. The process of recruitment began with advertisements placed in international sociological journals at the end of 1944. Candidates were interviewed in the middle of 1945 by a panel in London, whose members included Radcliffe-Brown, Raymond Firth and Audrey Richards, and by one in South Africa, whose members included Mrs Hoernlé, Isaac Schapera, Hilda Kuper and Gluckman himself. Professor Melville Herskovits (1895–1963) acted as a consultant for the American applicants. By the time Max published a revised version of the plan in *Human Problems* in December 1945, the war had ended, four sociologists had been appointed, and one for Southern Rhodesia, J.F. Holleman (1915–2001), who was funded by the Beit Trust, had already arrived. Two of the other three were on their way to Africa (Gluckman 1948: 59–74; Brown 1979: 533–39).[3]

There is not space here to summarize the lengthy plan, but it began with a typically bold statement:

> This plan for co-operative, co-ordinated, social research in British Central Africa is the first plan of the kind in the British empire. It aims to analyse the organization of modern

Central Africa and to show how selected urban and tribal African Communities live within it. We hope in carrying it out both to analyse the scientific relations present in this situation, and to provide the people participating in it, Government, Africans and others, with accurate intelligence of what is happening. (Gluckman 1945b: 1)

In the introductory section, Gluckman made a strong case for advances in sociology – he did not say social anthropology – over the previous twenty years and for its status as a specialist skill. It may have been a matter of debate with provincial commissioners, and others, but he insisted that the institute must be independent of government so that it could be critical of policy. It could, of course, be responsive to government concerns, and several of the most important of these had been presented to Gluckman by the Secretary for Native Affairs. There was a need for investigation of various aspects of social change in Northern Rhodesia, especially industrialization with labour migration, and stabilization or urbanization. The work of earlier social anthropologists, including his own, 'all demonstrate that it is industrialization with labour migration which dominates the whole trend of social development . . . Clearly, then, since this system of organising dominates the whole economic development of the country and the social organisation of all its parts, all social problems must be studied within its embrace' (1945b: 7). He also looked to the future:

as part of this study we shall analyse the formation of new groups and relationships, in both urban and rural areas; to achieve this it is necessary to regard mines and stores, district officers and missionaries, as factors in modern Central African Society which function in the same society as Native smithies and exchange-in-blood-brotherhood, as chiefs and magicians . . . I must emphasise that I do not view the social processes at work as entirely disintegrative . . . The problems set for the urban areas alone indicate my awareness that new groupings and relationships, perhaps torn by conflicts, are emerging. (1945b: 9)

The plan proposed that there was a need for sociologists to work in a variety of contrasting areas, industrial and nonindustrial towns, a cash-cropping area and people, with a focus on the Tonga of the southern province, a labour-supplying area such as the eastern province, with a focus there on the Chewa, Tumbuka and Ngoni, and a fishing area, such as the Luapula. There would be a need for cooperation and comparison in research and writing between sociologists working in these different areas. There was no immediate need for further work among the Lozi, or the Bemba, where he and Audrey Richards had worked.

Although Gluckman won the Royal Anthropological Institute's 1945 Wellcome Medal for the plan, there was little theory in it. He did, however, provide a survey of the ethnographic work that had been done in Northern Rhodesia up to that date, and he posed questions in relation to urbanization and 'detribalization', which drew on his Zulu experience, and his visit to Lozi migrants on the South African mines – they were to be a continuing concern. He thought that the concepts of 'urbanization and detribalization needed further refining'. In a passage that anticipated his later (1956) catchphrase 'An African miner is a miner; an African townsman is a townsman', he wrote:

> For example, in a sense every African is detribalized as soon as he leaves his tribal area, even though he continues to be acted on by tribal influences: he lives in different kinds of groupings; earns his livelihood in a different way, comes under different authorities. Does the influence of tribal culture decrease progressively the longer a man is away from his tribe? I have evidence from the Zulu to show that this is certainly not a definite correlation. We must draw a series of correlations of this type, between periods of residence in the town: family ties, tribal culture, political loyalty to the tribe, etc., etc. By the combination of planned urban and rural research, it should be possible for our team to do this from both ends of migration of men from the rural areas to towns. (1945b: 12)

The plan also envisaged the eventual recruitment of other specialists, as in demography, medicine and nutrition, psychology and linguistics, administration and history, and law, as well as co-operation with the government's technical experts in education, agriculture, veterinary science and labour. Gluckman seemed to envisage that he would have to do some of the urban research himself, though he was less than enthusiastic, preferring rural fieldwork. He had been down a South African goldmine in 1943, but he does not appear to have shown any interest in the Northern Rhodesian copper mines. He referred in the plan to his own expertise in law and was to follow up some of the legal questions posed in the plan in his later work on Lozi jurisprudence.

Gluckman published a popular, and illustrated, version of the report in *Libertas* in March 1946 under the title 'Human Laboratory across the Zambesi'. This emphasized the scientific basis of sociological research and its practical usefulness in relation to issues such as labour migration. The article was accompanied by a dramatic map, which graphically illustrated the relative volumes of migrant labour flows from the different provinces of Northern Rhodesia, from Barotseland to the Zambesi Sawmills at Mulobezi and to the South African mines, and from the northern, eastern and Luapula provinces to the Copperbelt (This map is reproduced in Gordon 2018: Figure 17).

Harking back to the 'Analysis', Gluckman was at pains to point out that Northern Rhodesia, like South Africa, was a single society and that the RLI researchers would be interested in all its members:

> Though all our officers are to work in African rural areas or among Africans in towns and industries, this does not mean that we attach undue importance to African problems as such. We realise full well that Europeans, Indians and Africans are all members of a single community. They affect each other's lives at every point. Just as the Europeans depend on Africans for labour in industries, shops and farms, and in their houses, so the Africans depend on Europeans

to prevent inter-tribal wars, and to teach them the culture of the Western civilization that is now spreading through the world. (Gluckman 1946: 39)

Much of Gluckman's language was reminiscent of the 'Analysis' with its references to force and the power of government:

The power of Government dominates all. It has vastly superior force, skill and organization. Above all it represents the money and the goods which are the chief common points of interest between Europeans and Africans – though they are also the chief points of conflict. In many ways, the District Commissioner is now more important than the chief. (1946: 39)

Gluckman had a good deal to say about the ill effects of labour migration, but he noted that 'the picture is not entirely one of disintegration. While native society is subject to stresses and tensions, new forms of social organization are emerging'. He concluded:

I began by warning you that we are studying 'only' Africans. 'Only' is incorrect. For since Europeans and Africans in Central Africa form a single society, in studying the modern African, we are also studying his fellow citizen. the European. Our studies hope to provide all sections of the country with scientific analyses of social problems affecting them, and such analyses must be available for sound development. (1946: 49)

Gluckman's celebrated Seven-Year Plan may have been accepted in principle by the RLI's board of trustees in 1944–45, but it was never funded as such. When the Governor, Sir Gilbert Rennie (1895–1981), opened the RLI's new headquarters in Lusaka in October 1953, after its transfer from Livingstone, he stated in a speech that must have been written for him by the then director, Clyde Mitchell (1918–95), that Dr Gluckman and his successor, Dr Colson, had in 1947 'worked out a co-ordinated five-year research scheme for the Institute . . . The five-year scheme was approved at the end of 1949, and its first year of operation was 1950'. In fact, as will be shown in more detail below, the institute operated under a funded four-year plan from 1946 to 1949, and a further funded five-year plan from 1950 to 1954 (RLI 1954: 3–4).

THE RECRUITS ARRIVE

Gluckman was determined that the new recruits should be thoroughly trained in African social anthropology, and he supplied them with reading lists and contacts before they left for Africa. His appointment committees had clearly done excellent work and the standard of recruits was high, as was demonstrated by their later careers. The three sociologists, recruited for the institute in terms of the plan, were John Barnes (1918–2010), a Cambridge graduate who had served in the Royal Navy from 1940 to 1945 and been awarded the Distinguished Service Cross, Elizabeth Colson, a graduate of the University of Minnesota, with a Ph.D from Radcliffe who had already done research on Native Americans, the Makah, and J.C. (Clyde) Mitchell, a graduate of the University of Natal who had served in the South African Air Force from 1942 to 1945. The reserve was Max Marwick, a social psychologist, also a University of Natal graduate, who was awarded a Colonial Research fellowship, independently of institute funding. J.F. Holleman (1915–2001), a University of Stellenbosch graduate, the Beit Trust fellow for Southern Rhodesia, came from a different sociological tradition – that of *volkekunde*. His previous publications were in Afrikaans and he seems to have largely escaped Gluckman's influence and control, though, unlike Marwick, he did attend the RLI conference in Livingstone in 1947 (Gluckman 1948 and addendum giving biographies of the recruits).

The plan envisaged the appointment of an economist. G.L. Unsworth was appointed, but he did not arrive. The gap was filled by the fortuitous appointment by the Colonial Office of Phyllis Deane (1918–2012), a protegée of John Maynard (Lord) Keynes

(1883–1946), who was sent out to draw up national income estimates, the first ever compiled for African colonies, for Northern Rhodesia and Nyasaland. She worked very closely with the RLI's sociologists in 1946–47 – to mutual advantage – and became the author of *Colonial Social Accounting* (1953), which was based on her work in Northern Rhodesia and Nyasaland. She had entirely positive memories of Gluckman, who she remembered as charismatic and inspirational. She visited him in Barotseland during his final period of fieldwork there in 1947. She also remembered, fondly, the RLI seminars that he held on the banks of the Zambesi above the Victoria Falls (Phyllis Deane, interview, 1993).

Barnes, Mitchell, Max Marwick and his wife Joan arrived in Livingstone in January 1946 and were immediately rushed off by Gluckman to Ndola for an introduction to fieldwork in a Lamba resettlement area. He also introduced them to his friends, the ecologist Colin Trapnell (1907–2004) and the agriculturalists David Peters and William Allan. By March, they had transferred to Cape Town, where he gave them a lengthy course with the help of Professor Isaac Schapera and of Professor G.P. Lestrade in African languages. While in Cape Town, they were also introduced to Jack Simons, who gave lectures on urban studies, and they visited the scene of his urban research in Langa and other townships. In Johannesburg, they were introduced to most of Gluckman's intellectual network, including Mrs Hoernlé, Hilda Kuper and Ellen Hellman, as well as the demographer Dr Henry Sonnabend, the psychologist Wulf Sachs, Professors Doke (African languages), J.S. Marais (history) and I.D. MacCrone (psychology), Julius Lewin (Native law and government) and J.D. Rheinallt Jones, then of the Institute of Race Relations (Gluckman 1948; Schumaker 2001: 85–91).

Elizabeth Colson joined the group in Cape Town in May. Her departure from the United States had been delayed by the Northern Rhodesian Governor's failure to book her a ticket. She eventually set off from San Francisco in April in a cargo ship, which, unusually, sailed around Cape Horn. Gluckman met her at the docks in Cape Town and she later recalled her first impressions:

He was very tall, very bald, and his energy was apparent from the beginning. Max had tremendous energy. Indeed, I used to think in later years that he was the kind of person who exhausted all the oxygen in the area immediately around him. But he was also a very generous man, which I learned later. He was also very political at that point. (Elizabeth Colson, online interview, 2002)

Colson believed him when he said he had never joined the Communist Party, though others said that he had done so: 'He presented his ideology as . . . pro-African, which we thought was a good ideology.' Asked whether he was a communist or a socialist, Colson said she didn't think he could tell the difference. Somebody in the colonial service had jokingly told him: 'Max, you are an anarchist imperialist, or an imperialist anarchist.' Colson, an American with no stake in the British Empire, thought that 'he had a tremendous amount of belief in the British system and thought that it was going to deal honestly, over the long run, if properly guided, with the Africans. And that was what I think he really cared about' (Elizabeth Colson, online interview, 2002).

Gluckman acknowledged in his director's report that, contrary to his expectation, Colson was 'well-grounded in African anthropology' and did not need further training. She had expected to go to Luapula and was a little disappointed when he told her that she would be going to the Tonga in the Southern Province because the provincial commissioner in Luapula thought that his Congo border area was too dangerous for a lone woman researcher. Meanwhile, she went to visit Monica Wilson at Fort Hare University College in the Eastern Cape, and she also visited the Transkei, before rejoining the group in Johannesburg. As the senior researcher, and the only one with a doctorate, she then assumed a leadership role in the absence of Gluckman, who had gone on leave to Britain (Gluckman 1948: 66).

Max Marwick, who initially fell out with Gluckman, though they were reconciled at a much later date, left with his wife for his fieldwork among the Chewa in the Eastern Province of Northern Rhodesia in June 1946. It was only in September that the other recruits set off for their research areas: Barnes to the Fort Jameson Ngoni in the Eastern Province, Colson to the Tonga in the Southern Province and Mitchell to the Yao in the Southern Province of Nyasaland. They were to remain in their respective areas for most of a year, though they returned to Livingstone for an RLI conference organized by Gluckman in January–February 1947, during which they all gave talks about their work. The conference was also addressed by the Wits demographer Henry Sonnabend and by Phyllis Deane. The group stayed in a hotel, met on the banks of the Zambesi, and talked all day and into the evening. Mitchell thought that the conference was most useful for the discussion of fieldwork methods. The conference set a precedent and was followed up almost annually for fifteen years. Colson and Barnes both visited Gluckman during his last period of Barotseland fieldwork, which was between March and July of that year. Mary Gluckman had given birth to their second child, Peter, in December 1946, and she seems to have spent the period of fieldwork with their two small children in Mongu rather than at Katongo. Phyllis Deane visited Colson, Barnes and Gluckman in the field in April–May and they all collected family budgets for her. The practice of circulating fieldnotes was also soon established and helped to establish a collegial atmosphere (Gluckman 1948; Schumaker 2001: 101–10).

GLUCKMAN'S RESIGNATION

The original plan was that after a year in the field the researchers would return to Livingstone for a year's writing-up from September 1947. In his director's report for 1943–46, which was prepared at the end of the latter year, Gluckman indicated that, because of shortage of accommodation in Livingstone, this might have to be done at a South African or a British university. At the time that he wrote this report, he had resigned and knew that he would be leaving the institute to take up a job at Oxford University in October 1947. He would be joining the Social Anthropology Department, which was headed by Evans-Pritchard and of which Fortes was a member. He had fixed up the job on his trip to England in July–August 1946. In the end, he left in August 1947 and Colson, Barnes and Mitchell followed him to Oxford in September of that year. He continued to act as director of the RLI until December 1947, when he was succeeded by Elizabeth Colson who was to hold the post from 1948 to 1951. Audrey Richards, who had made huge efforts on his behalf to secure funding for the expansion of the institute, was, understandably, furious about his resignation, as was the board of trustees, and the Colonial Social Sciences Research Council (CSSRC). They also disapproved of his plan to take Colson, Barnes and Mitchell with him for writing-up in Oxford (Gluckman 1948; Schumaker 2001: 110–11).

It does seem extraordinary that after all the work that he had done to raise funds for the institute, and to appoint and train staff, Gluckman should leave when he had only just managed to get the show on the road. He never seems to have made a clear statement about the reasons for his resignation. He had mended his fences with the government, he had done work for it and he apparently had a good relationship with the governor, Sir John Wadding-ton, but he had recurring problems with the board of trustees and had threatened to resign in 1945. He had at that time told Meyer Fortes that he would like a job at Oxford. He and Mary may also have been bored after six years of relative intellectual isolation, based in wartime, and small-town, Livingstone. It may not have been the best place in which to bring up a young family. Moreover, full-time administration did not leave him with much time to write up the notes that he had accumulated over a total of twenty-seven months of fieldwork in Barotseland over seven years. He may also have been daunted by the prospect of urban – presumably Copperbelt – research, to which he had commit-ted himself, but which he had not yet begun. He also told the CSSRC: 'I should get teaching experience or I should never be able to return to university life' (Schumaker 2001: 110; Gordon 2018: 298–301).

Elizabeth Colson's later accounts of Gluckman's period as di-rector of the institute from 1942 to 1947, and her own period as director from 1948 to 1951, published in *African Social Research* in 1977, make it clear, however, that there may have been other reasons for his sudden departure. Although she later denied that she felt deserted by Gluckman, she came close in these articles to suggesting that he had abandoned a sinking ship. The four-year funding for the research officers would come to an end in 1949. The funding was in any case inadequate because it took no account of rapid postwar inflation and made no provision for administrative costs, for the provision of cars, which researchers now expected, or for essential African assistants. The separation of the institute from the museum meant that the institute had to move out of the museum building, and it ended up sharing a 'ramshackle' – her word – wooden building with the Department of African Education. The institute's office space had been halved and was now reduced to three rooms, including the library and the director's office. The library books were finally shared with the museum in 1948. The capital fund had also been split between the two institutions, and the institute's share had to be spent on administrative costs in 1946–48. Gluckman was supposed to have started a fundraising drive before he left, but he had failed to do so. He had effectively left the institute 'in cold storage with only a part-time, recently appointed, secretary book-keeper and a typist to keep things going in Livingstone' (Colson 1977a: 285–95; Colson 1977b: 297–307; Colson, online interview, 2002).

When Colson returned as director to Livingstone from Oxford in June 1948, she had to start again from scratch. There was no accommodation in Livingstone for research officers and the government had taken back the director's house when Gluckman left. She spent much of 1948–49 working on a new Seven-Year Plan – she had produced a draft by November 1948 – and on funding applications to the Colonial Social Science Research Fund and the Beit Trust. She had to combine this hard administrative work with her Tonga fieldwork, as there was no provision for her accommodation in Livingstone, and inadequate provision for her salary as director. Fortunately, she could travel easily by train from Monze, a station near her research area, to Livingstone, and she did so every month or two. She also travelled occasionally to Lusaka for meetings of the board of trustees. She got help in fundraising from the new governor and chairman of the trustees, Sir Gilbert Rennie, and by the end of 1949 they had secured £100,000 from the Commonwealth Development and Welfare Fund. There was also some additional funding from the Northern Rhodesian government and from the mining companies. This was enough for a five-year plan, to begin in 1950, and included £29,000 for new buildings. (Colson 1977a: 285–95; Colson 1977b: 297–307; Colson, online interview, 2002).

Livingstone had become a backwater, and Rennie pressed for a move to Lusaka. Colson had some reservations about this because the institute was intended to be regional, not national, and she thought that the location of the institute at Northern Rhodesia's capital might increase demands from government on staff time, but she chose a site near Munali Secondary School, about five miles from the centre of Lusaka. She hoped that the institute could recruit research assistants from Munali and she anticipated, more or less correctly, that it would be the site of a future university.[4] Construction began in 1951 and the institute moved in 1952. As an economy measure, Rennie chose an off-the-peg design for a district headquarters, or *boma*, for the new building. This may have surprised, or possibly alarmed, African visitors from rural areas, and confirmed the view of those who, somewhat unfairly, saw the institute as an extension of the provincial administration. Among those present at the opening of the new institute in 1953 was Davidson Sianga, still Gluckman's part-time research assistant, though he had other duties. He was probably then the institute's longest-serving employee. Desmond Clark, curator of the museum since 1937 with a long wartime break, was also there, but he was no longer linked to the institute. Monica Wilson, widow of the founding director, was also in attendance, but neither Gluckman nor Colson was present (Colson 1977b: 297–307; RLI 1954: 3–4).

NOTES

1. Gluckman spelled Mwendawelie with a final 'e', but it is now spelled with a final 'i'.
2. This appendix did not meet with universal approval in government. In a review of *Essays on Lozi Land and Royal Property*, clearly written at Gluckman's request, his friend Eric Unsworth, a legal officer, recommended readers to ignore or tear out this appendix. (*Human Problems in British Central Africa*, 2, 1944, 68)
3. In his report on the institute for 1943–46, Gluckman states that the recruitment process, with interviews, took place in 1944, but this must be a misprint or mistake.
4. The University of Zambia was founded in 1966 on a site on the Great East Road about a mile from the institute.

CHAPTER 4

FROM OXFORD TO MANCHESTER

• • •

Gluckman spent only two years at Oxford working as a senior lecturer in Evans-Pritchard's department. Much of his time in the first year was spent with Barnes, Colson and Mitchell, the three research officers from Northern Rhodesia. Barnes and Mitchell were accepted for doctoral studies at Oxford with Evans-Pritchard and Fortes at this time. Gluckman also recruited a fourth officer, Ian Cunnison, while in Oxford, and gave him some initial training. He later told Lyn Schumaker that the 'Analysis' was central to his training: 'It was the Bridge, the Bridge, the Bridge, all the time the first few years' (Schumaker 2001: 78). He was to undertake research in the Luapula area, as had been specified in the Seven-Year Plan. Like Barnes and Mitchell, he eventually completed his D.Phil. in Oxford. He later joined Gluckman's department in Manchester as a sociologist in 1955 and stayed until 1959. Marjorie Elliot, who was to do a macrostudy of labour migration from Nyasaland and the Rhodesias, was also recruited in Oxford in 1948.

During this time, Gluckman, Barnes, Colson and Mitchell drafted four of the seven articles that were to appear in *Seven Tribes in British Central Africa*. This was co-edited by Gluckman and Colson and was the first book to be produced by the RLI. The manuscript was submitted to Oxford University Press in 1949 and the book was published in 1951. These articles on the Lozi, Ngoni, Tonga and Yao were based on lectures that they gave to the Institute for Social Anthropology seminar in Oxford. Gluckman's contribution to *Seven Tribes* was a 100-page monograph on the political and social organization of the Lozi. Mitchell thought that the book should have had an introduction, and Elizabeth Colson regretted the use of the word 'tribe' in the title – it was not a word that she used herself in her essay on the Plateau Tonga, but Gluckman continued to use it for many years (Colson 1977b; and author's conversations with Elizabeth Colson).

Barnes, Colson and Mitchell also gave lectures on contemporary political developments among the Ngoni, Tonga and Yao to the joint LSE and University College, London, social anthropology seminar, which was run by Raymond Firth and Daryll Forde. These articles were published in *African Studies*. While in Oxford, Gluckman, Barnes and Mitchell also read papers to a joint meeting of the Royal Anthropological Institute and the International African Institute in May 1948 under the title 'The Village Headman in British Central Africa'. They were published under that title in *Africa* in the following year. They also gave a joint broadcast on the BBC Third Programme (Colson 1977b: 297).

As early as April 1949, Gluckman was able to tell Monica Wilson that he had been offered a professorship at the Victoria University of Manchester in what was a new Department of Social Anthropology/Sociology. He had applied for a readership, but after a 90-minute interview with a large group of academics, he was offered the professorship. The interviewing panel included several recently appointed professors in the social sciences, some of whom were to become Gluckman's friends and to participate in his social anthropology/sociology seminar. These were W.J.M. (Bill) Mackenzie (1909–96) in politics, Ely Devons (1913–67) and W. Arthur Lewis 1915–91) in economics, and Michael Polanyi (1891–1976) and Dorothy Emmett (1904–2000) in philosophy. Lewis was a West Indian and the first Black professor at a British university. He was later awarded the Nobel Prize for Economics (Foreman 2014: 105).

It is not quite clear why Gluckman had become so quickly restless at Oxford, but Evans-Pritchard encouraged him to move on as a means of spreading his own influence. Whether in Oxford or Manchester, Gluckman was anxious to maintain his links with Africa and the RLI. He continued as a co-editor of *Human Problems*, and he also continued to publish his own Rhodes-Livingstone papers. He also retained a nominal connection as a consultant. He was able to maintain a strong link with the RLI so long as two of his recruits, Colson and Mitchell, were in charge, which was the case until 1955. Colson carried on the tradition that he had started of RLI conferences. Her first was held at the Central African Archives in Salisbury, Southern Rhodesia in December 1948, and her second in Bulawayo in the following year (Colson 1977b: 299–301). A telegram sent by the participants from the Salisbury conference demonstrated their loyalty to Max in suitably anthropological language:

> Addressing ancestral spirit Annual rite at brain shrine Please accept beer libation demonstrating solidarity descendents [*sic*] No fragmentation stop Please confer structural clarity as heretofore – Clyde [Mitchell], Elizabeth [Colson], Hans [Holleman], Ian [Cunnison], John [Barnes], Margery [Marjorie] Elliot. (From photograph reproduced in Gordon 2018: Figure 18)

The practice of research officers travelling to Britain after a year in the field for writing-up was also continued and new recruits, under Colson's watch, were sent to Oxford or Manchester (mainly the latter) for initial training. These included A.J.B. Hughes, who was recruited in 1948, with Beit Trust funding, to study the Ndebele of Southern Rhodesia. After a year in Oxford, he arrived in the field late in 1949 or early in 1950. Victor Turner (1920–83), a Scottish graduate of University College London with war service, was recruited in 1950 and spent a year in Manchester. He was originally intended to work with the Mambwe-Lungu of the Northern Province of Northern Rhodesia, but he was encouraged by Gluckman to take on the Lunda-Ndembu in the Mwinilunga district of the North-Western Province of Northern Rhodesia. According to his wife Edith, Gluckman told him that the Ndembu area was rich in yellow fever, and ritual, in which he, though a devout communist, was believed to have an interest.

He returned to Manchester to complete his Ph.D. with Gluckman in 1955 and then joined the department as a lecturer, staying
there until 1962. He was unhappy when the department began
undergraduate teaching in 1960 and left soon afterwards. The
Ndembu area did indeed prove to be rich in ritual (Turner 2006:
58). Widely believed to be the most brilliant of the RLI recruits,
his books included: *Chihamba the White Spirit: A Ritual Drama
of the Ndembu* (1962), *The Forest of Symbols: Aspects of Ndembu
Ritual* (1967), *Schism and Continuity in an African Society* (1968)
and *The Drums of Affliction: A Study of Religious Processes among
the Ndembu of Zambia* (1968).

William Watson (1917–94), a Scottish graduate of Cambridge
with a distinguished wartime career in the Royal Air Force (RAF),
was also recruited by Colson in 1950 and took on the Mambwe-
Lungu. He did a year's training with Gluckman in Manchester
and returned there after fieldwork, like Turner, to complete his
Ph.D. with him. He also joined the department and stayed until
1963. Lewis Gann (1924–97), a German Jewish refugee in Britain
who served in the British army in Germany at the end of the war,
was an Oxford history graduate who was recruited by Colson
in 1950 as the institute's first and only historian. He spent a year
with Gluckman before joining the institute in 1951. It is not clear
whether he finished his doctorate, but after a year in Northern
Rhodesia, he spent two years in Manchester in 1952–54, before
taking a job at the Central African Archives in Salisbury.

Marian Pearsall had been recruited to work among the Lakeside Tonga of Nyasaland and did the Manchester training, but she
dropped out soon after her arrival in Africa in 1951. She was replaced in 1952 by Jaap van Velsen (1921–90), an Indonesian-born
Dutch student of Gluckman's in Oxford and Manchester, who
completed the study of the Lakeside Tonga. He also completed his
Ph.D. in Manchester. It was published by Manchester University
Press in 1964 as *The Politics of Kinship: A Study in Social Manipula-
tion among the Lakeside Tonga of Nyasaland*. In 1971–73 he was to
serve briefly as director of the RLI's successor, the Institute of African Studies, within the University of Zambia (Colson 1977a: 285–
96; 1977b: 297–308; Mitchell 1977: 309–18; Gann 1993: 482–83).

Arnold L. (Bill) Epstein (1924–99) joined the RLI at the end of 1952 to undertake the long-delayed Copperbelt urban research. A law graduate of Queen's University, Belfast, who had done some social anthropology at the LSE, he had come to Northern Rhodesia in 1950 on a Colonial Social Research fellowship to do work on the Urban Native Courts system on the Copperbelt. He registered for his Ph.D. with Gluckman at Manchester and completed it in 1957. The resulting book on Luanshya, *Politics in an Urban African Community* (1958), was, like Clyde Mitchell's *Kalela Dance* (1956), directly inspired by Gluckman's 'Analysis'. He also became a lecturer in the department and remained there until the mid-1960s. While doing his doctoral work in Manchester, Epstein met and married T. Scarlett Grunwald (later Epstein), who did social anthropological work in India.

All these personal links between Gluckman, the RLI and Manchester were forged within a few years of his arrival at the university, and they were maintained over the years. Elizabeth Colson went on leave to the United States in 1950, intending to return to Northern Rhodesia to supervise the building of the new institute in Lusaka, but she was diagnosed with anaemia and decided she could not return to Africa. Clyde Mitchell succeeded her as director of the RLI in 1951–52, and she became a Simon Fellow and then a senior lecturer in Gluckman's department from 1951 to 1953. She left Manchester for family reasons, but also because she thought she would like to have 'more ability to develop outside the overwhelming influence of Gluckman'. She was offered jobs by Evans-Pritchard in Oxford and by Raymond Firth in London, but she thought that if she had taken a job elsewhere in Britain, Gluckman would have seen that as a 'defection' or 'base treachery' (Colson, online interview, 2002; Colson, online interview, 2006).

Gluckman had invited Clyde Mitchell to come to Manchester in 1950, but he preferred to renew his contract with the RLI. He spent time on leave in Manchester in 1953, but when he left the institute in 1955, he decided to take a job as a professor of sociology in the new University of Rhodesia and Nyasaland in Salisbury. A.L. (Bill) Epstein was Gluckman's preferred candidate to succeed Mitchell in the directorship of the RLI in 1955, but the latter realized that Epstein would be opposed by the white settler community. Like Godfrey Wilson before him in Broken Hill, Epstein had been excluded from research work in the mine compounds in Luanshya on the Copperbelt in 1952, and the board of trustees regarded him as politically dangerous. Much to Gluckman's fury, they appointed Henry Fosbrooke, a civil servant from Tanganyika and a 'safe pair of hands'. Mitchell was appointed to a professorship in social anthropology in Manchester in 1960, but he decided to stay in Southern Rhodesia. Mitchell finally came to Manchester as a professor of urban sociology in 1966, but only after the Rhodesian Unilateral Declaration of Independence (UDI) in November 1965. He arrived in Manchester as tension between the disciplines of social anthropology and sociology, and between Gluckman and Peter Worsley, was growing, and he was not happy there. He moved to Oxford in 1973, soon after the split in the department, which finally took place in 1971 (Mitchell 1977: 309–18; Mitchell papers: Gluckman-Mitchell correspondence, 1951–59; David Boswell, interview).

MORE RLI–MANCHESTER LINKS

Gluckman was able to dispense patronage to RLI members and other friends with the help of the Simon Fellowships. These were funded primarily for the benefit of the economic and social science faculty by Lord Simon of Wythenshawe (1870–1960), a wealthy Manchester industrialist and Labour party peer, and his wife, Sheena Potter (1883–1972), a suffragist and philanthropist. The Simons had been introduced to each other by the founding Fabians, Sidney and Beatrice Webb. After her husband's death, Lady Simon gave their home, Broomcroft at Didsbury, to the university for the accommodation of academic visitors. Among the RLI researchers who received Simon fellowships were Elizabeth Colson in 1951, John Barnes in 1952–54 for work on Norway, and Max Marwick in 1962 for writing up his work on Chewa witchcraft, which was published as *Sorcery in Its Social Setting* by

Manchester University Press in 1965. Gluckman also secured a Simon fellowship for his friend William Allan, the government agriculturist, in 1959–60. This enabled Allan to write his classic book *The African Husbandman* (1965). He also found fellowships for several friends who had been involved in training the RLI's first recruits in South Africa. Hilda Kuper came in 1958. Jack Simons, who, with his wife Ray was forced into exile after being banned from university teaching, came in 1965. A two-year fellowship enabled them to complete their classic book *Class and Colour in South Africa* (1969) and Jack to finish his classic text *African Women: Their Legal Status in South Africa* (1968). Another friend and South African exile for whom Gluckman found a fellowship in 1967 was Julius Lewin, who came with his wife, Eleanor Hawarden. The trade unionist E.S. 'Solly' Sachs, father of Albie Sachs, had come earlier in 1952–54 (University of Manchester 1972).

The Simon Fund provided not only for research fellowships and visiting professorships, as for A.R. Radcliffe-Browne in 1950 and 1951, but also for visiting lectures. In 1959, Emrys Peters, acting as head of the Department of Social Anthropology, invited Evans-Pritchard, Forde and Fortes to deliver Simon lectures in the following year. Forde and Fortes both spoke about aspects of ritual, while 'E.P.' spoke about anthropology and history. Forde's lecture on Yakö mortuary ritual and Fortes's lecture on 'ritual and office in tribal society' were brought together with Victor Turner's seminar paper on 'Three Symbols of *Passage* in Ndembu Circumcision Ritual' and Gluckman's introductory overview, 'Les Rites de Passage', in *Essays on the Ritual of Social Relations*, which was published by Manchester University Press in 1962. In his preface to the book, Gluckman paid tribute to Lord Simon, who had recently died: 'As soon as he realized that anthropologists dealt with general problems of social life, his lively interest in all things human was awakened and characteristically he followed the development of the work with great sympathy' (Gluckman 1962: vi).

It was not only social anthropologists, and refugees and exiles from Southern Africa such as Simons and Lewin, who benefited from Simon funding. In 1956 Gluckman invited the Marxist historian Eric Hobsbawm (1917–2012) to give three Simon Lectures on the Lazarettists, a nineteenth-century Italian millenarian movement. From these lectures there emerged in 1959 Hobsbawm's first major work, *Primitive Rebels: Studies in Archaic Forms of Social Movement in the Nineteenth and Twentieth Centuries,* which became a classic. He acknowledged that without Gluckman's encouragement, the book would 'certainly not have been written'. He also recalled discussions at what was apparently a weekend seminar in Manchester, chaired by Gluckman, with other experts on millenarian movements, including Peter Worsley and Norman Cohn. Worsley's book on cargo cults in the New Hebrides, now Vanuatu, *The Trumpets Shall Sound,* was first published in 1957, as was Cohn's book on mediaeval millenarian movements, *The Pursuit of the Millennium* (Hobsbawm 2017: xi).

The Simon Fund also provided for visits to Manchester by a series of distinguished American sociologists, demonstrating, as Lewis Gann noticed, Gluckman's openness to American scholarship. The first visiting professors were two of Gluckman's near contemporaries, Edward Shils (1910–95) in 1952 from Chicago and George Homans (1910–89) in 1953 from Harvard. They were followed by the younger Erving Goffman (1922–82), who came as a visiting professor twice in 1963 and 1966–67. According to Elizabeth Colson, Talcott Parsons (1902–79) came for a term, but his name does not appear in the list of Simon visiting professors (Colson, online interview, 2006).

MANCHESTER UNIVERSITY PRESS

Another important link between the RLI and Manchester came through Manchester University Press. Gluckman's *magnum opus, The Judicial Process among the Barotse of Northern Rhodesia,* was published by the Press in 1955. It also published his 'Analysis' in pamphlet form in 1958 on behalf of the RLI. Clyde Mitchell's *The Yao Village: A Study of the Social Structure of a Nyasaland Tribe* was published by the press on behalf of the RLI in 1956. Elizabeth Colson's *Marriage and the Family among the Plateau Tonga of Northern Rhodesia*, William Watson's *Tribal Cohesion in a Money Economy: A Study of the Mambwe People of Northern Rhodesia*, Lewis Gann's *The Birth of a Plural Society: The Development of Northern Rhodesia under the British South Africa Company, 1890– 1924* and A.L. Epstein's *Politics in an Urban African Community* were all published for the RLI in 1958. Ian Cunnison's *The Luapula People of Northern Rhodesia; Custom and History in Tribal Politics* came out in 1959. All these books carried forewords by Gluckman, and there were more to follow in the 1960s.

THE SOCIAL ANTHROPOLOGY/ SOCIOLOGY SEMINAR

The departmental seminar, which Gluckman usually chaired, acquired a frightening reputation as a bit of a bearpit. Fredrik Barth's biographer, T. Eriksen, put it mildly when he wrote that the seminar was 'not known for its politeness when outsiders came to present their research'. The seminar's members 'had a reputation as earthy, pragmatic, sharp and polemical intellectuals'. Barth (1928–2016) came to speak in 1956–57 as a student at Cambridge of Edmund Leach who was known to be 'Gluckman's main antagonist in the small, tight world of British anthropology', but the seminar went 'reasonably well' (Eriksen 2013: 93). Barth himself provided a good outsider's description of the seminar and its chairman:

> Gluckman had an unusual ability to wrestle directly with the ethnographic data of others as presented in their papers and he used it with great skill during seminar discussion. What emerged under the label 'extended case method' was the collective fruit of such skills. To visitors, presenting a paper at Manchester would always be a stimulating challenge. To regulars these presentations sometimes took on the character of a blood sport. 'You could positively see him

wilt' was the triumphal report I heard of one such session.
(Eriksen 2013: 93)

Barth concluded that '[t]he whole Manchester group was driven
in those years by the enormous vitality of "Max" and his intrinsic
engagement with the thought, indeed the total lives, of all members of the gang'. Raymond Apthorpe (born 1932), who worked
at the RLI from 1957 to 1960, might well appreciate the last noun
in that sentence. He had to be ushered away with a bloodied nose
by a postgraduate student after an assault by Bill Watson after his
only appearance at the seminar, which he describes as pugilist,
in 1962 (Barth 2005: 38; Raymond Apthorpe, interview, 2022).

Ronnie Frankenberg, in his foreword to Edith Turner's memoir *Heart of Lightness*, recalled the early 1950s and a less formal
and more friendly atmosphere in 'the almost continuous seminar
in Max's office and other offices in the Dover building', as well as
in local 'caffs' and 'the informally annexed TV room in the academic staff club across Oxford Road' (Frankenberg 2006: xix).

THE MANCHESTER SCHOOL OR 'SCHOOL'?

Given this range of RLI-Manchester connections and all these
publications, as well as the large body of RLI publications produced in the previous fifteen years or so – about thirty papers,
thirty numbers of *Human Relations* and a score of communications – it is hardly surprising that Mary Douglas, who had
encountered Gluckman in Oxford, should, when reviewing Watson's *Tribal Cohesion in a Money Economy* in the journal *Man*,
have commented:

> From the many and illuminating references [in this book]
> to the researches of other Manchester and Rhodes-Living-
> stone anthropologists, whether they have worked in cen-
> tral Africa or other fields, it is evidently time to salute a
> school of anthropology, whose publications are developed

through close discussion, and where each worker's work is enhanced by his focus on a common stock of problems. (Douglas 1959: 168)

This brief book review, which acknowledges 'Professor Gluckman's admirable foreword', is usually credited with christening Gluckman's 'Manchester School', or what he apparently preferred to describe as the 'Manchester "School"'. Douglas was not actually referring to a 'Manchester School', but to a 'Manchester-Rhodes-Livingstone School' of social anthropologists. There was, by 1959–60, no comparable group of social anthropologists, nor any comparable mass of publications, dealing with any region of Africa or the world.

In an undated manuscript, written in circa 1963, entitled 'History of the Manchester "School" of Social Anthropology and Sociology', Gluckman gave his own account of the emergence of this 'school', tracing its genealogy in direct line of descent to his Manchester seminars from the Oxford seminars for RLI researchers in 1947 and the first of the RLI conferences held on the banks of the Zambesi in the same year. He describes that as 'the conference where we all came out of our tribes and met at Livingstone, [where] we worked out a coordinated attack on common problems by similar methods and techniques'. He continues to describe a diaspora of RLI people to universities around the world and anticipates, given the funding for which he is appealing, a resurgence of Central African research based on Mitchell's chair at the University of Rhodesia and Nyasaland – an indication that he had by then abandoned the RLI after the Epstein debacle and the Fosbrooke takeover (quoted in Schumaker 2001: 252–53).

It appears that both Douglas and Gluckman himself were thinking of a 'network', as much as a 'school'. Network was, of course, a social anthropological concept that was pioneered by Meyer Fortes, and then developed by John Barnes and promoted by Clyde Mitchell, within the Manchester tradition. Douglas may also have been hinting at an incestuous coterie, a group of scholars who mainly quoted each other. She must have noticed that, as well as a foreword by Gluckman, William Watson's book on the Mambwe carried almost a score of references to Gluckman's work, including no fewer than four to the 'Analysis', nine to Mitchell's work, seven to Barnes's and three to Colson's (Watson 1958).

In his masterly survey of postwar departments of anthropology *Anthropology and Anthropologists: The Modern British School*, Adam Kuper (born 1941) emphasizes the dictatorial powers of the professoriate and tends towards a view of the 'Manchester School' as a coterie, if not an actual 'tribe'. He describes the progress of members of the school from RLI fieldwork through writing-up to doctorates, to Simon Fellowships and to lectureships in the department. He suggests that '[far] more than anywhere else, a single line dominated the department'. He does not refer to Gluckman's demand that all staff members and postgraduate students should ritually attend Manchester United football matches, but he does quote the joking refrain, one might say maxim, 'We are all Maxists here'.[1] In his summary:

> The department had close links with some departments abroad and, later, in the north of England, which became parts of the Manchester 'empire'. As soon as a member of the fellowship was appointed to a post elsewhere, he tried to surround himself with other Manchester men. Manchester school publications often cited only other members of the school. Collections of essays edited by one of the faithful normally included only essays by other members. A characteristic example is Epstein's *The Craft of Social Anthropology*, published in 1967. Its list of contributors reads like a roll-call of the Manchester School-Max Gluckman, Elizabeth Colson, Clyde Mitchell, John Barnes, Victor Turner, Jaap Van Velsen, A.L. and T.S. Epstein, and Max Marwick. Other members of the school who did not work in Central Africa (and so, perhaps, were judged to be lacking in the craft of social anthropology) were Ronald Frankenberg, Emrys Peters and Peter Worsley. Loyalty to Max was demanded from everyone. In the macho and par-

anoid atmosphere that Gluckman fostered, dissidents were treated with great ferocity. (Kuper 2015: 98)

In Elizabeth Colson's view, it was more of a 'Manchester approach' than a 'Manchester School'. In her review of Evens and Handelman's edited collection on *The Manchester School,* she noted that the contributors wrote of:

> social networks, the extended case method, situational analysis, and the social drama as the defining characteristics of Manchester, but these were neither unique to, nor invented at, Manchester. Gluckman himself advocated rather than used them, for his fieldwork after 1947 was confined to a brief revisit to Barotseland in 1965. (Colson 2008: 335)

In Colson's recollection, the most distinctive characteristic of Manchester was 'the probing discussion of whatever anyone was working on which at times seemed to be regarded as a joint enterprise'. She thought that Gluckman, influenced by Marx and his experience in Southern Africa, was interested in what would later be called 'globalization'. He 'stressed the transformative effects on even the most remote village of industrialization, international markets and increasing control exercised by centralizing governments'. Following Godfrey Wilson, he was more interested in 'individuals making decisions rather than social structures composed of interconnected social roles'. She thought that Gluckman's own research interests were 'eclectic and empirical... He was not interested in theory for theory's sake'. He knew something of Freud, but he thought that psychology was irrelevant to social anthropology. The Manchester interest in social networks had originated with her own reading of George Homans's *The Human Group* (1951), as a result of which Gluckman had invited him to Manchester for a term, and Gluckman's own interest in case studies was derived from E.A. Hoebel and Karl Llewellyn's *The Cheyenne Way* (1941). (Colson, interview, 2002; Colson 2008: 335–37).

THE FEDERATION OF RHODESIA AND
NYASALAND AND GLUCKMAN'S EXCLUSION
FROM NORTHERN RHODESIA

Gluckman's excuse for not doing further fieldwork in Barotseland and writing his promised third monograph on Barotse jurisprudence, a book on the courts, was that he discovered from a
senior member of the government of the Federation of Rhodesia and Nyasaland, which had been set up in 1953, that he would
be denied entry to Northern Rhodesia. This may not be a totally
convincing excuse as there is no reason to believe that he would
have been prevented from entering Northern Rhodesia between
1947 and 1953, or that he contemplated entering the country between 1953 and 1957, but he does seem to have been excluded
from the country from the latter date. Gluckman took the matter
up informally in August 1957, with his wartime friend, Sir Roy
Welensky (1907–91), who had become Prime Minister of the
Federation in 1956. He told him that he 'could do with a barge
trip on the Zambesi and some duck shooting' and that he was de-
bating between spending a year in California or a year in Rhodesia, 'assuming of course that I will get an entry permit!' Welensky
feigned surprise at the suggestion that he might be denied entry.
He forwarded what must have been a more formal letter from
Gluckman to the Minister of Home Affairs in October, and the
matter was discussed at a high level, but there was apparently no
change. When Clyde Mitchell invited him to visit the University
College of Rhodesia and Nyasaland in Salisbury (now Harare)
in 1958, he replied to say that he had been 'tipped off by a high
source that it would be "inadvisable" for me to try to go into the
Federation"' (Oxford: Welensky papers: Gluckman-Welensky
correspondence, August 1957, and private secretary to the Prime
Minister to private secretary, Minister of Home Affairs, with an-
notations, 13 November 1957; Mitchell papers, Gluckman to
Mitchell, 13 December 1958).

There had, of course, been official concern that the Gluckmans were a security risk dating back to 1940. Gluckman organized meetings in Mongu, Barotseland, with Abe Galaun, a

Latvian-born (and Jewish) trader, in support of the Soviet Union after it joined the war in 1941, and he was well informed about the inner workings of the Communist Party of South Africa in the late 1940s. He and Mary were close to Frank Maybank, the New-Zealand-born, but Australian and communist, leader of the Northern Rhodesian Mineworkers' Union who was deported to the United Kingdom as a security threat in 1942. They were so close that their links were investigated by the special branch at that time. The families remained in touch over thirty years and following Maybank's death in the early 1970s, his family sent his personal papers to Gluckman for onward transmission to Zambia, but they have since disappeared (RAI. Gluckman papers: Gluckman to Tommy Fox-Pitt, 29 July 1948; Money 2016: 40–41; Macmillan and Shapiro 2017: 184–85).

Gluckman was not outspoken in his opposition to the establishment of the federation, but he corresponded with Tommy Fox-Pitt (1897–1989), whom he had befriended when he was acting provincial commissioner in Barotseland, based in Mongu, in 1946–47. After his retirement in 1951, Fox-Pitt remained for a while in Northern Rhodesia and became an ally of Simon Zukas (1925–2021), a young Lithuanian-born civil engineering graduate who was involved with the predominantly African, and radical, Anti-Federation Action Committee, while working for the municipality in Ndola. He was arrested early in 1952 and held in prison for eight months in Livingstone pending deportation. He had a high-powered legal defence team, but he was deported at the end of the year to the United Kingdom, a country with which he had no previous connection. Fox-Pitt corresponded with Gluckman in 1951 about Zukas, who the Northern Rhodesian special branch and MI5 linked with Bill Epstein for no other reason than that they were both radical and Jewish. Fox-Pitt himself left Northern Rhodesia at the end of 1952 and became secretary of the Anti-Slavery Society, and a leading member of the radical Movement for Colonial Freedom, which was founded in London in 1954 (RAI. Gluckman papers: Fox-Pitt to Gluckman, 25 July 1951, 5 September 1951; Macmillan 2000: 102–4; Macmillan and Shapiro 2017: 263).

Max and Mary, with Elizabeth Colson, attended a protest meeting against the federation in Manchester in January 1953, which was addressed by the Reverend Michael Scott (1907–83), and chiefs from Northern Rhodesia and Nyasaland, who were touring the country to campaign against it. Scott was the founder, though not the chairman, of the Africa Bureau, which he had set up in June 1952 with the primary objective of opposing the federation. Following this meeting, Mary was recruited to help organize a second meeting and was actively involved in setting up the Manchester and District Council for African Affairs, which was closely associated with the Africa Bureau, though not formally affiliated with it. Mary became the secretary of the council, which declared itself to be nonpolitical and nonsectarian, and she was clearly its prime mover. According to lengthy annual reports, which she produced for 1953 and 1953–54, there were further meetings during 1953 that were addressed by Dr Hastings (Kamuzu) Banda (circa 1896–1997), then a doctor in London, and a conference that was addressed by Michael Scott, Tommy Fox-Pitt and Phyllis Deane. The conference brought together 200 delegates from 100 local organizations, including churches, and produced a petition with 2,500 signatures calling for the postponement of federation until African consent could be obtained. By the middle of 1953, it was clear that the federation was going to go ahead, but the council resolved to remain in existence to campaign on other African issues and on race relations in Manchester and the surrounding district, where there were an estimated 4,000–5,000 'Coloured' people (Mitchell papers: Elizabeth Colson to Clyde Mitchell, 27 January 1953; Africa Bureau papers: Manchester and District Council file, Mary Gluckman, annual reports, 1953, and 1953–54).

The first chairman of the council was Bishop J.L. Wilson (1897–1970), the former Bishop of Singapore and a survivor of the Japanese prisoner-of-war camps, who was the Anglican Dean of Manchester until his appointment as Bishop of Birmingham. Gluckman did not take a leading part in the council and, according to Elizabeth Colson, he 'had honestly tried to restrain himself' politically. Arthur Lewis was a vice-president of both the council and of the Africa Bureau, and he became the chairman of the sub-committee on race relations in Manchester. Later speakers included Solly Sachs (1900–76), a Simon fellow, and Anna Scheepers (1914–99), both leaders of the South African Garment-Workers Union (Mitchell papers: Elizabeth Colson to Clyde Mitchell, 27 January 1953; Africa Bureau papers: Manchester and District Council file, Mary Gluckman, annual reports, 1953, and 1953–54).

After the federation, the next major African issue was Kenya, with which Max became publicly involved. Mary reported on the formation of the Movement for Colonial Freedom in 1954, but she was not its first secretary, as was apparently suggested in her *Guardian* obituary, nor was she actively involved with it. The council could not be associated with the movement because of its own nonpolitical status. Mary corresponded with Michael Scott, Mary Benson (1919–2000), secretary, and Jane Symonds, assistant secretary, at the Africa Bureau and reported on events in Northern Rhodesia, including the 1953 Lusaka butchery boycott, which resulted in a climbdown by the butchers and the ending of segregated counters (Mitchell papers: Elizabeth Colson to Clyde Mitchell, 27 January 1953; Africa Bureau papers: Manchester and District Council file, Mary Gluckman, annual reports, 1953, and 1953–54; Africa Bureau papers: Mary Gluckman to Mary Benson, 11 March 1954).

Max may not have been conspicuously active, but he attended public meetings and Mary's activism must have been noted by MI5, and through it by the British Security Liaison Office, Central Africa, in Salisbury, and by its successor, the Federal Intelligence and Security Bureau (FISB). They both kept a close eye on the Reverend Michael Scott, Dr Banda and the Africa Bureau. British McCarthyism, and 'screening' for communists, a phrase used by Gluckman in correspondence with Clyde Mitchell, seems to have become more prevalent after the election of a Conservative government in 1951. The federal government was clearly determined to keep Gluckman out of the country and to reduce his influence on the RLI. The trustees did this by blocking the appointment of Bill Epstein as director. He was also later blocked for appointment to Mitchell's department at the University of

Rhodesia and Nyasaland. Known or alleged communists, such as Ronald Frankenberg (1929–2015) and Peter Worsley, both Max's Ph.D. students, were blocked for appointment to the RLI and for other African posts. The exclusion of Frankenberg from research for Manchester in St Vincent in the Windward Islands, and his deportation from Barbados in 1952, became political issues and were eventually debated in the House of Commons in 1954 (Mitchell papers: Gluckman to Mitchell, 19 December 1956; Yates and Chester 2006: 128, 134–35; Foreman 2014: 83–89).

Frankenberg's effective exclusion from British colonial Africa and the British West Indies had significant consequences for the 'Manchester School'. He was virtually compelled to undertake a British topic and began work in 1953 in a village in North Wales close to the border with England. By his own account, his fieldwork site was forced on him by Manchester University Vice-Chancellor Sir John (later Lord) Stopford's insistence that he should work no more than a day's journey from Manchester, and by Gluckman's insistence that he must learn a 'foreign' language. The resulting book, *Village on the Border: A Social Study of Religion, Politics and Football in a North Wales Community*, was published to considerable acclaim in 1957. Frankenberg himself saw it as an example not only of 'auto-anthropology', a word coined by Marilyn Strathern, in which the researcher worked within his or her own society, but also as an example of 'participant observation' – a phrase that he claimed to have coined himself in a magazine article in 1963. He credited Gluckman's 'Analysis' as a pioneering example of 'auto-anthropology' in relation to South Africa (Frankenberg 1989: 169–93; Foreman 2014: 95).

Gluckman's involvement in a public spat with Sir Philip Mitchell, the former governor of Kenya, following an article in the *Manchester Guardian*, which was followed up by a BBC Third Programme broadcast in April 1954, did not help his profile in Southern Africa, where he could be portrayed as an apologist for Mau Mau. His argument was that Mau Mau was in no way an atavistic reversion to 'savagery', as was widely believed in official circles, but was a modern political phenomenon, for which there were well-known socioeconomic causes, but for which there was no precise precedent. Gluckman appeared once or twice, at a later date, on a Movement for Colonial Freedom platform with Peter Worsley and Tom Mboya (1930–69), the prominent Kenyan nationalist leader (Gluckman 1963: 137–45; Worsley 2008: 124).

Gluckman did, of course, make his own contribution to ensuring his exclusion from contact with the RLI. He was furious that Raymond Apthorpe and John Argyle were appointed to the institute after interviews in London in 1957 to which he was not invited. He was further angered because they were not advised to see him before leaving for Africa. He convinced himself that Fosbrooke was turning the institute into an 'adjunct' to government. His attitude was somewhat irrational as Fosbrooke had shown no prejudice against Gluckman or his former colleagues. He had recruited Elizabeth Colson in 1956 to work on the social consequences of resettlement for the Tonga of the Gwembe Valley as a result of the construction of the Kariba Dam and the flooding of the valley. This was work that she carried out with Thayer Scudder in what became a sixty-year longitudinal study. Gluckman contemplated resigning as a consultant to the RLI in 1957 and finally did so in a fit of fury in March 1959. Fosbrooke, presumably thinking that Gluckman would change his mind, tactfully 'lost' the letter, and Gluckman, receiving no acknowledgement of it, wrote directly to Sir John Moffat, the president of the institute's trustees. While telling Clyde Mitchell that he would not correspond with any RLI staff members, including the young Raymond Apthorpe who had been sending him papers, he was not entirely consistent. He did not resign from the editorial board of *Human Problems in British Central Africa* (Mitchell papers: Gluckman to Mitchell, 8 April, 8 August 1957, 4 September 1959, Gluckman to Fosbrooke (copy), 21 March 1959, Mitchell to Gluckman, 18 July 1959)

PUBLIC INTELLECTUAL: *CUSTOM AND CONFLICT*

Gluckman's intervention on Kenya, and his broadcast on that topic in April 1954, helped to turn him into a well-known public intellectual. He had a real talent for broadcasting, which he had first shown in Northern Rhodesia during the war, and he gave about a dozen broadcasts on the Third Programme in 1954–55. As Peter Worsley noted:

> Max prided himself, rightly, on his style as a writer, preferring short, Anglo-Saxon words to long Latinate ones. His manuscripts were covered with crossings-out where he tried one adjective after another. This lucidity gave him the ability to communicate with readers other than anthropologists, notably on the radio. His talks on the highly prestigious Third Programme of the BBC, mostly about quite obscure anthropological topics, such as witchcraft, were immensely popular but never 'dumbed down'. (Worsley 2008: 76)

The most remarkable of these were the six 7,500-word lectures that Gluckman delivered in the spring of 1955. They were published by Basil Blackwell in 1956 as *Custom and Conflict in Africa*, which was his most popular book. Gluckman acknowledged that the producer, Michael Stephens, helped him to work out the theme of the talks and chose the title. They were exceptionally long – three times the length of the usual Third Programme talks. The titles of the lectures were all paradoxical: 'The peace in the feud', 'The frailty in authority', 'Estrangement in the family', 'The logic in witchcraft', 'The licence in ritual' and 'The bonds in the colour bar'.

The first of these is, perhaps, the best known. It is a rewriting of Evans-Pritchard's work on fission and fusion among a stateless people – the Nuer – and it illustrates one of Gluckman's main themes: conflict and cohesion. The second lecture draws on Gluckman's own work to illustrate similar themes in the Zulu and Lozi kingdoms. It includes, incidentally, a joke at his own expense – a list of the desirable attributes of professors. They should be, but might not always be, 'learned and scholarly, original research-workers, inspiring teachers, tolerant with students, and good administrators' (Gluckman 1956: 27). The third lecture looks at the differences between patrilineal and matrilineal kinship systems in Africa, but also refers to Elizabeth Bott's ongoing work on kinship networks in the East End of London. The lecture on witchcraft relates mainly to Evans-Pritchard's work on the Azande, but also refers, as one of Gluckman's wartime broadcasts did, to racial stereotypes, Nazism and the Jews. The lecture on the 'licence in ritual' deals with rituals of rebellion and refers to Gluckman's own work on the Zulu and to Hilda Kuper's work on the Swazi, quoting three *Ncwala* songs. The final lecture was a popular rewriting of the 'Analysis of a Social Situation in Modern Zululand', with an update to take account of the later imposition of apartheid. His later book *Politics, Law and Ritual in Tribal Society* (1965) was also published by Basil Blackwell and aimed at a nonacademic audience, but it was more technical and lacked the immediate accessibility of *Custom and Conflict*.

CONFLICT AND COHESION

In many ways *Custom and Conflict* summarized Gluckman's intellectual position as it was in 1955. As Peter Worsley pointed out, Gluckman's department had something that other departments did not have – 'a coherent theoretical position'. As he wrote in his own memoir:

> The analysis of the 'social situation', and not solely of large-scale structures, was also one of his methodological emphases. More widely, to him, conflict was basic in any society or social situation. Those who were opposed in one sphere might, however, be aligned with quite other people and have different opponents in other spheres. Divisions in one sphere 'cut across' divisions in another, and these did not overlap so as to form one absolute kind of generalised opposition across the whole social order. These cross-cutting ties and overlaps made possible the overall persistence, even the integration, of the social order. And since there were many kinds of social opposition, no one of them

(such as class struggle) was any more determinant or 'ultimate' than any other. (Worsley 2008: 76–77)

This was not, however, a position that was compatible with orthodox Marxism. Worsley added, somewhat wryly, that he and Ronnie Frankenberg were inoculated against it by their Marxism.

TOWARDS THE END OF FEDERATION

Gluckman's most significant political intervention came in January 1960 when he submitted a thirty-two-page memorandum to the Monckton Commission, which had been set up by the British government to consider the future of the Federation of Rhodesia and Nyasaland. He followed this up with oral evidence to the commission in London on 25 May 1960. Harold Macmillan's 'winds of change' speech to Parliament in Cape Town and the Sharpeville Massacre both took place between these two dates. His written presentation consisted largely of an essay, later published, on 'tribalism', urbanization and industrialization in Central Africa. It drew on his own work, on Mitchell's *Kalela Dance* and on Watson's work on the Mambwe. In his oral evidence he insisted that it had been a mistake to impose the federation without African consent and he predicted that, without radical political change in the federation, there would be increased violent resistance and 'Sharpeville after Sharpeville'. He supported universal suffrage, after some hesitation over universal female suffrage, and did not think that this would 'shatter the state' any more than it had done in Britain. He thought that 'the alternative is that you cut the poor and illiterate off from all sources of political power except violence, and in practice it is the poor and illiterate who need the vote much more than the rich and the educated' (Monckton Commission 1960: 134–35). The Monckton Commission's report recommended radical political reform for Northern Rhodesia and Nyasaland – it could not make a recommendation for Southern Rhodesia. Its conclusions on the north infuriated Sir

Roy Welensky and signalled the end of the federation, though it survived until 1963.

NOTE

1. David Boswell, who was in the department in the 1960s, recalls: 'Max expected his staff and research students to attend Manchester football matches. Having declared to myself freedom from compulsory sport once I left school, I did not attend them.' David Boswell to Hugh Macmillan, email, and interview, Oxford, 7 July 2022.

CHAPTER 5

THE JUDICIAL PROCESS AMONG THE BAROTSE AND *THE IDEAS IN BAROTSE JURISPRUDENCE*

●   ●   ●

For the first decade or so that Gluckman was in Manchester, he did little or no undergraduate teaching. Most of his university work involved postgraduate teaching and running the departmental seminar. He devoted a great deal of his energy over nearly twenty years to the production of two substantial monographs in legal anthropology, which were based on his fieldwork in Barotseland in the 1940s and that he had begun writing in Oxford. These books appeared as *The Judicial Process among the Barotse in Northern Rhodesia* (1955) and *The Ideas in Barotse Jurisprudence* (1965). A third volume, *The Role of Courts in Barotse Life*, was planned, but was never written. Its completion would have required additional fieldwork, which he was unable to undertake because of his exclusion from the federation, though it cannot be said that he had shown any enthusiasm about returning to Barotseland for a decade after his departure in 1947. From 1955 onwards, he established an international (especially American) reputation as a legal anthropologist and theorist. This was based on fieldwork that he had done in Northern Rhodesia, but he acquired a new and a wider audience. He had moved into an intellectual territory, which he had first encountered when reading Sir Henry Maine's *Ancient Law* as a student of Mrs Hoernlé at Wits in 1929–30.

Figure 5.1. Gluckman's photo of the court and council building at the *Litunga*'s capital, Lealui, 1940. © RAI. 400. 043299

The Judicial Process was a big book, which was first published in 1955 with close to 400 pages. It ended up, after the addition of two new prefaces, a 'Reappraisal' (1966), which reviewed the book's reviews, and an account of his return to Barotseland in 1965–66, at 500 pages on its third iteration in 1973 (Gluckman 1973a). The heart of the book, about half its core content, consists of transcripts and analyses of sixty-five court cases, mainly appeal cases, heard at the Lealui *Kuta* in 1942, when Gluckman began his research on the Lozi legal system, and in 1947, when he did his last fieldwork in Barotseland. The majority of these, extending to as many as ten printed pages each, were Gluckman's own records of cases. Some were recorded by his research assistant Davidson Sianga, while others were relatively brief texts, taken from the Lealui *Kuta* records. With titles like 'The Case of the Contemptuous Husband', 'The Case of the Quarrelsome

Teacher', and 'The Case of the Violent Councillor', they are indexed as in a standard English legal textbook.

Gluckman was studying what is called 'customary law', but he was conscious that he had been living and working in a country that was undergoing rapid social change. He was also conscious that Lozi judges, who were largely concerned with marital disputes and cases involving property, had to take account of issues like the impact of labour migration and absentee husbands. He was also aware that the customary courts were undergoing rapid change as a result of pressure from the colonial government. They had been deprived early in the colonial period of most criminal jurisdiction and they were no longer able to order customary punishments, such as flogging. When he began work on the topic in 1942, the courts were coping with the recent (1936–37) introduction of Native Authorities, a feature of Indirect Rule. On his last fieldwork trip in 1947, further changes involving the closure of some courts – the *kutas* – and a reduction in the number of judges, had just been introduced.

When Gluckman gave his four broadcast talks in 1954 on the themes of the about-to-be published book, he gave them the title 'The Reasonable Man in Barotse Law'. He boasted that he had managed to reduce his book to 11,000 words and that his talks had received a high approval rating. An American friend, apparently George Homans, had commented: 'You have reached the top now. All that is left is a long, slow, coast downhill.' In the first of the talks, he had explained his title.

> I can still recall vividly how I was sitting in my deckchair listening to a trial in a Barotse Court, when I recognized an old friend. He is inscribed in huge letters on the blank page opposite my notebook's record of the process of examination: 'Hullo, the reasonable man!' (Gluckman 1963: 178–9)

Gluckman acknowledged that he had listened to many court cases in Barotseland and Zululand, but he had for long been blind to 'the existence of this basic figure of [English] jurisprudence in African law'. Once he had observed him in 'The Case of the

Violent Councillor', he was able to reconsider all the cases he had heard as 'exhibitions of his [the Reasonable Man's] dominant role in the judicial process':

> I came to appreciate that he was the means by which the judges applied the fixed rules of general law and morality to the general circumstances of Barotse life. Above all, he was the means by which they adjusted these fixed rules to cope with the great changes which the Barotse's life is undergoing as they are absorbed in the modern world. (1963: 178–9)

The crux, and the most controversial part of the book, was his conclusion that:

> On the whole, it is true to say that the Lozi judicial process corresponds with, more than it differs from, the judicial process in Western society. Lozi judges draw on the same sources of law as Western judges, the regularities of the environment, of the animal kingdom, of human beings; and custom, legislation, precedent, equity, the laws of nature and of nations, public policy, morality. They assess evidence in the same way. They manipulate the different types of legal rule which can be applied, and the ambiguity of the concepts which make up the legal rules, in a similar attempt to achieve justice according to their lights. (Gluckman 1973a: 357)

Gluckman did, of course, acknowledge that there were also differences, for example, in levels of technology, in the social and economic structure of Lozi society, which was relatively egalitarian and undifferentiated, and in 'the absence of pleadings and counsel and complex procedure, and the unwritten state of the law'. In his 1966 'Reappraisal', he considered no less than fifteen reviews and review articles dealing with the book. He noted that at least four of the reviewers – J.G March, T.H Marshall, Mary Douglas and V. Ayoub – emphasized the differences rather than

the similarities between the judicial systems. He also referred
to Paul Bohannan's *Justice and Judgement among the Tiv* (1957),
which raised the question of whether Tiv legal concepts had English legal equivalents. There were suggestions by various commentators that Gluckman had forced Lozi legal concepts into
English or, through his own legal training, Roman-Dutch legal
categories. He acknowledged that he might have been better advised to list the similarities and differences, and not to suggest
that the similarities were greater than the differences, but he defended himself against the suggestion, which he described as a
'myth', that he had 'jammed' Lozi concepts into Roman-Dutch
categories (Gluckman, 1973a: 377). He also had to contend with
objections, for similar reasons, to his use of the 'Reasonable Man'
concept.

Gluckman's emphasis on similarity may have provoked controversy among his fellow anthropologists, but he had a fundamental belief in the similarity of cultures and the processes by
which they functioned. He attributed this to growing up in South
Africa and to his opposition to segregation and apartheid, and
stated it forcefully, as has been indicated above, in his posthumously published essay on 'Anthropologists and Apartheid'. The
comparability of 'primitive', or 'tribal' law with both 'ancient'
and modern Western law, was what interested both British and
American students of jurisprudence in Gluckman's Lozi work.
He asked A.L. Goodhart (1891–1978), the American-born former professor of jurisprudence at Oxford (1931–51), who was
then Master of University College, Oxford (1951–63), to read the
manuscript of *The Judicial Process*. After doing so, Goodhart re-
sponded by writing a generous foreword in which he commented
on 'the fundamental similarity between the administration of
justice in Loziland and in Great Britain or the United States'. He
concluded that:

> No legal philosophy, however pure or abstract, will in the
> future be able to disregard the facts which he has presented
> in so clear and convincing a manner. It will be many years

before a more interesting and a more path-breaking book is published in the field of political science. (Gluckman 1973a: xvi–xvii)

In October 1960 Gluckman was invited to give the prestigious Storrs Lectures at Yale Law School and he delivered them in April 1963. He was only able to deliver, over two weeks, short versions of four of the eight lectures that he had prepared, but the complete series was published in 1965 by Yale University Press as *The Ideas in Barotse Jurisprudence*. He said that the title was derived from a chapter heading in Gibbon's *Decline and Fall of the Roman Empire* and that the book might more accurately have been entitled 'Footnotes to Sir Henry Maine's *Ancient Law*' – an essential theme of which was the legal progress 'from status to contract'. The book did not deal as much with Lozi case law as its predecessor had done, but it did grapple with English medieval history and law in comparison with Lozi custom on issues such as the distinction between rebellion and treason. He summarized the contents of the book as dealing with 'the law of the constitution and the theory of power; treason and royal succession; the nature of rights in land; the different laws applying to movable and immovable property; concepts of property, of contract, of wrong and injury, and of debt' (Gluckman 1972a: xv–xviii).

THE AMERICAN IMPACT

Charles L. Black (1915–2001), Henry Luce Professor of Constitutional Law at the Yale Law School and a civil rights lawyer who was involved in *Brown v. The Board of Education* the landmark Supreme Court case that outlawed school segregation in 1954, wrote the foreword to the new book. He described Gluckman's impact on the law school:

he was copious of apt and accurate citation, flowing with ideas, the thorough-paced academic humanist whose com-

mand of his own specialty was evidently the fulcrum of a
lever aspiring toward the length of Archimedean dream
and solidly reaching a very long way. It is to be doubted
that anybody else ever made such an impression on the
Yale Law School in two weeks. He left behind him a buzz of
talk as to when we might get him to come back. (Gluckman
1972a: ix)

Gluckman was invited back to Yale three times in the next decade, for the last time in 1972.

Charles Black had some interesting things to say about the
book. He questioned whether, in the light of what Gluckman
had written about Lozi jurisprudence, and the intricacies, for example, of the 'case of the Fisherman's Net', the old distinctions
between 'early' and 'late' or 'primitive' and 'civilized', law could
any longer be sustained. Taking up the issues of allegiance, rebellion and treachery, he drew an analogy with the contemporary
campaign for civil rights, and the question of state rights, in the
United States:

> Though the structural problem is not the same, it may not
> be long before we in the United States have to consider
> similarly searching questions about the exact direction of
> allegiance, for the Negro community in one or more of our
> states may be driven into total civil disobedience to state
> authority, while seeking no quarrel with the nation, and
> the rest of us will have to consider whether such an act is a
> rupture of the essential allegiance that binds us all together,
> or a mere 'rebellion', albeit peaceful, to rid the state of an
> unjust rule, and the nation of a state rule defiant of national
> order. (Gluckman 1972a: xii)

At the end of the Civil War, a similar decision had to be made
as to whether the Southerners were rebels or traitors. Black was
sure that the right choice was made because the Southern rebellion had been made 'under a claim of legal right asserted under
the federal Constitution itself'.

Black was also prompted, 'as a constitutionalist who knows nothing of Africa', to ask 'why it is that well-developed political structures such as the one Gluckman here describes seem to have been so little employed in building the modern governments of the new African states' (Gluckman 1972a: xii). This was a question that was to be raised again nearly thirty years later in Basil Davidson's *The Black Man's Burden* (1992). Black concluded his foreword with these words: 'It is a long time since legal anthropology has seen a book so thorough, so learned, so rich in thesis and allusion as *The Ideas in Barotse Jurisprudence*' (Gluckman 1972a: xii).

Elizabeth Colson, speaking in 1989 in Lusaka at a conference to commemorate the fiftieth anniversary of the founding of the Rhodes-Livingstone Institute, drew attention to the practical impact that Gluckman's Lozi work had in the United States. He had emphasized reconciliation, rather than punishment, as an objective of Lozi justice, and Colson pointed out that his work, and that of his colleagues, had 'provided models of dispute resolution based on a principle of restoring harmonious relationships that have had a profound impact on the American legal system. Neighbourhood tribunals based on such models have been set up to relieve the regular courts of their heavy caseloads'. New systems for alternative dispute resolution (ADR) were introduced in the United States in the late 1950s and early 1960s, and small claims courts were introduced in the United Kingdom at about the same time. Colson's friend Laura Nader (born 1930), a legal anthropologist, had some doubts about the applicability of this innovation 'on the grounds that what works well when contestants are tied together by multiple ties and mediation is carried out by neighbors with a stake in the outcome can work abominably when contestants are an aggrieved person demanding redress from a powerful corporation or powerful landlord' (Colson 1992: 9). Colson, on the other hand, noted that 'it is significant that the Institute's decision to sponsor research in Western Province 50 years ago has been relevant to the development of the American legal system' (Colson 1992: 9; Nader 1988: 269–91).

THE BAROTSE NATIONAL OR SICABA PARTY

In his preface to *The Ideas in Barotse Jurisprudence* written in June 1964, Gluckman showed himself to be aware of the rise of African nationalism in Northern Rhodesia/Zambia and its impact on the Lozi monarchy, which had flirted with the federal government and, though he did not say it, with a separate independence. The *Litunga*, Sir Mwanawina III (died 1968), had, with the political backing of Sir Roy Welensky and the United Federal Party, and the financial backing of the British South Africa Company, launched the Barotse National Party, also known as the Sicaba (Nation) Party, to contest the pre-independence elections on a 'traditionalist' and secessionist platform. Its leader was Induna Francis Suu, one of Gluckman's closest Lozi friends and collaborators, and one of only two men whose photographs appear in *The Judicial Process* – the other is Induna Solami Inete. His photograph had also appeared in Gluckman's 1945 article in *Libertas* on the Zambesi River kingdom, where he was described in the caption as a 'Progressive councillor – one of the most powerful men of the Barotse Nation'. He would eventually become *Ngambela*, though in a much-diminished kingdom. 'Traditionalism' had little popular appeal, and Kenneth Kaunda (1924–2021)'s party, the United National Independence Party (UNIP), won all the seats in Barotseland in the elections in November 1962. Bulozi remained a protectorate within a protectorate until the eve of Zambia's independence in October 1964, when its incorporation with Zambia was negotiated through the Barotse Agreement. This was a tripartite agreement, negotiated in London, between the United Kingdom, self-governing (but not yet independent) Northern Rhodesia, and the *Litunga* on behalf of the Barotse Council and people (Macmillan 2005: 239–45).

Gluckman discovered when he returned to Barotseland, which was by then the Barotse Province, in 1965 for the first time in eighteen years that there had been a serious deterioration in the productivity of the central plain, and its margins, and a large increase in the population dependent on it. Furthermore, the post-independence government, which had no love for the Lozi monarchy, had by then abolished the *kutas* and restricted the powers

Figure 5.2. Gluckman's photo of Francis Suu, his good friend, senior Lozi councillor and later *Ngambela*, Barotseland, 1940. © RAI. 400.030985

of the Lozi councils to land distribution. According to Meyer Fortes, in his article on Gluckman in the *Dictionary of National Biography*, it was his dismay at the situation in postcolonial Barotseland that encouraged him to devote all his energies to research on Israel. By the time that he paid his last brief visit to Zambia in 1972, the UNIP government had, in 1969, unilaterally revoked the Barotse Agreement and Barotse Province had been renamed Western Province (Gluckman 1973a: 419–45; Fortes 2004).

A CRITIQUE OF GLUCKMAN'S LEGAL ANTHROPOLOGY

In his preface to *Cross-Examinations: Essays in Memory of Max Gluckman* (1978), a symposium dedicated to Gluckman's legal anthropology, P.H. Gulliver regretted that this had been neglected by both social anthropologists and students of jurisprudence. His 'legal materials, and his conclusions, have been on the edges, a minority interest'. Writing a decade before Elizabeth Colson's essay, which highlighted the impact of his work in the United States, Gulliver thought that his influence in that country had been exaggerated. He concluded that Gluckman had 'not only contributed more than any other single anthropologist to the study of law in its widest sense, but in so doing he helped by the stimulus of his example to build up a new body of literature which, more than ever before it is folly to ignore' (Gulliver 1978: xvi).

In her essay 'Archaic Law and Modern Times on the Zambezi' in the same collection, Sally Falk Moore (1924–2021) was more critical. Looking at his two big Lozi books, she saw Gluckman's perspective, as, under the influence of Marx, Maine and Durkheim, an 'historico-evolutionary' one. Gluckman had been unable to write his promised third book on the Lozi courts because he did not have adequate fieldwork material. Ironically, the inadequacy of his fieldwork had become apparent to him because of advances in fieldwork technique that he had himself promoted through the RLI. His use of case studies followed Llewellyn and Hoebel's work on the Cheyenne, but it was also innovative in its use of live cases as opposed to oral tradition. He set out to show that the logic of African judges was not different from the logic of European courts. Writing on the eve of African independence when Europeans were casting aspersions on African competence, he sought to show how wrong they were. Like much of the work of other South African anthropologists, his work had a political purpose (Moore 1978: 53–77).

Yet, Moore argued, there was a problem. Gluckman was using Barotse law as an example of 'archaic' law – Maine's 'ancient' law or 'tribal' law. He provided some evidence for British colonial intervention and the modernization of customary law, but he was reverting to conjectural history (my phrase) in seeking to reconstruct a 'pristine tribal kingdom' (Moore's phrase). The courts of the 1940s were in no sense 'traditional'. The British had banned ordeals and divining, and had removed most criminal jurisdiction from the *kutas*. Gluckman had noted how much of the time of the courts was taken up with divorce cases, but, in another article in the same collection, Elizabeth Colson pointed out that the royal courts had only become involved with divorce cases by decree of the *Litunga* and the council in 1918. Marriages had previously been seen as private contracts. Colson thought that Gluckman had 'underestimated the extent to which Lozi marriage law and the attitudes of Lozi judges reflected the assumptions of British colonial administrators and British magistrates' (Colson 1978: 24–25).

In much the same way as Clarence-Smith had been critical of Gluckman's history, Moore was critical of his sense of time – with his mix of the 1940s and the reconstructed 'tribal' model. She suggested that he was using three kinds of time, 'then, now, and then-and-now'. She also took issue with his use of the 'Reasonable Man' concept, which she saw as timeless and unspecific as to content. It was a universal concept showing that African law shared basic features with other legal systems, but it was also a synthesizing term for several Lozi judicial concepts, such as 'the good husband' or 'the good councillor' (Moore 1978: 74).

Moore acknowledged that Gluckman was following Maine in examining the relationship between the legal system and society, and in asking basic questions about history and explanation that 'are at the heart of the social sciences'. He sought 'customs', but he was 'a pioneer in collecting data on *events*'. She thought that '[it] was a signal advance in legal anthropology that he did not turn Barotse law into a catalogue of rules, but had tried to show it as a working set of ideas and actions and processes' (1978: 76).

Moore concluded her essay with a quotation from Gluckman's *Ideas in Barotse Jurisprudence*, which she saw as a challenge for the future:

> My analysis of Barotse reasoning is woven out of these cases and if anyone feels that I have allowed my framework to be dominated by my comparative approach, the cases are there for analysis by anyone with a different approach. (Gluckman 1972a: 382–83)

A somewhat later commentary on Gluckman's *Judicial Process* is provided by Martin Chanock in his *Law, Custom and Social Order: The Colonial Experience in Malawi and Zambia* (1985). Chanock acknowledged that the book had 'ushered in modern African studies of legal anthropology' and that it was 'the most influential of the Rhodes-Livingstone studies in the field of law.' However, he did not think that it was the most illuminating. He included three times as many references to Elizabeth Colson's work as to Gluckman's in his book. He thought that Gluckman's observations on the actual Lozi legal process were of greater value than his discovery of rationality and international comparability in these processes. He noted Gluckman's conclusion that Lozi law was dominated by status, not equality, and that 'natural justice aims to maintain the established system of social positions and the ideas that justify the system'. Lozi customary law, as it emerged during the colonial period, defended the legal superiority of men in relation to women and the existing hierarchy. Gluckman had found that women among the Lozi were at all times in 'legal tutelage'. In the absence of writing, Chanock observed, 'the Lozi treat fairly recent innovations as ancient custom' (Chanock 1985: 29–30, 39).

THE AFTERLIFE OF GLUCKMAN'S
IDEAS IN BAROTSE JURISPRUDENCE

It was Gluckman's analysis of 'the nature of rights in land' that proved to have the longest-lasting significance. He maintained that the basic principles of Barotse landholding were 'that rights to land are an incident of political and social status'. In *The Ideas in Barotse Jurisprudence*, he developed the ideas that he had first outlined in 1943 in his essay on 'Lozi Land Tenure' about 'estates of administration and production'. While making many comparisons in the book with early English law, he was concerned to show that the Lozi system, though monarchical, was different from the medieval feudal system (Gluckman 1972a: 78–94). Soon after the publication of the book, Gluckman was asked by the International African Institute to chair a conference on African customary law, which was held at Haile Selassie I University in Addis Ababa in 1966. He gave a paper to the conference on 'Property Rights and Status in African Traditional Law', which went over some of the same ground. Starting from the position that a false antithesis was often made between the 'communistic' and the 'individualistic', he made a distinction between ownership, administration and production. The Lozi king was nominally the owner of the land, but he had an obligation to give land for use to all his subjects. He gave primary rights of administration, not ownership, to village headmen, who gave secondary rights of administration to heads of families, who in turn gave tertiary rights of production to family members. Land was not communally owned and if it was not used, it reverted backwards up the hierarchy of 'estates of administration' for re-allocation. Obligations flowed in both directions, and different people, and people of different statuses, could have rights over the same land for different purposes (Gluckman 1969: 252–65).

Given Gluckman's wartime interest in the applicability of the Soviet concept of the collective farm to Northern Rhodesia and his interest in individual rights in the collective, it is remarkable that social anthropologists working in the USSR on actual collective farms in the 1960s and 1970s, and on decollectivization in Romania in the 1990s, should have found his work on landholding and property in Barotseland relevant. In his Huxley Lecture at the British Museum in 2019, 'Economy and Ethics in the Cosmic Process', Chris Hann showed how Caroline Humphrey (Lady Rees of Ludlow, born 1943, wife of the Astronomer Royal, Lord Rees) in her monumental book *Karl Marx Collective: Economy, Society and Religion in a Siberian Collective Farm* (1983) adapted Gluckman's analysis of African land tenure to depict the collective farm in Buryatiya (southern Siberia) as 'a complex hierarchy in which rights over people were more important than rights over things'. She 'showed that the political economy of central planning depended on actors' negotiation of "manipulable resources" rather than market signals'. Through their retention of 'traditional gifting practices and Shamanism, the Buryats had managed to integrate novel socialist institutions into their traditional worldview' (Hann 2022: 5–29).

Caroline Humphrey understood Gluckman as arguing that:

> in precapitalist societies the individual's rights depend on his social status, or to put it another way, there is a series of overlapping rights over the same bit of property and that this hierarchy of rights is defined by the hierarchy of social relations (in the case of the African kingdom he was discussing: members of households, household heads, village headmen, chiefs of tribes, king). It is by virtue of membership of social groups, whose relation to the land differs at different levels, that each subject is entitled to claims over property, not as in capitalist society, where accumulated individual property and possession of money gives people social and political privilege. (Humphrey 1983: 118–19)

Writing about Soviet collective farms in what is now the Russian republic of Buryatia, Humphrey concluded that they should not be understood in terms of the classical Soviet analysis of the relations of production, and different types of ownership of the means of production, but rather in terms of Gluckman's analysis of Bulozi where an individual's rights to property depended on his or her social and political status. She suggested 'that in the Soviet Union too rights over the means of production, including labor, accrue to groups and individuals by virtue of their social-political status'. Using Gluckman's concept of 'estates' of administration and of production, she identified the former in the *kolkhoz* (the collective farm and its owners), the Party, and the Soviets, where she saw an overlapping hierarchy of rights in which an individual might have rights and powers in all three organizations. In terms of production, she identified a hierarchy of estates, ranging downwards from the chairman and management committee of the *kolkhoz,* through the brigadiers (leaders of brigades or subfarms), and the leaders of production units, to the workers (Humphrey 1983: 128).

Writing about decollectivization in Romania, Katherine Verdery (born 1948) made a similar use of Gluckman's concept of 'estates' of administration and production to explain the Soviet system. She quoted Humphrey on the use of the term *khozain* (proprietor or master) as being used at each level of the Soviet system. The directors of enterprises and the party bosses of districts and provinces were all called 'proprietors' and 'at the apex of the system Stalin in his time was called *nash khozain* – our master'. As Verdery elaborated:

> Just as the Lozi king allocated his rights downward without compromising his power, so the party-state retained its claim to supreme ownership but exercised that ownership by passing the rights downward to lower-level entities, assigning various kinds of control over parts of the property of the whole people to inferior levels in the bureaucratic hierarchy. Recipients of these rights could further parcel them out to others still lower down the scale...The heads of these lower units were to use the rights to generate products for the state to appropriate and redistribute. (Verdery 2003: 57)

The parallels appear to have been precise. As all property belonged to the state, transactions involving transfers of produce from one entity to another involved the transfer not of ownership, but rather of administrative rights. The socialist system had its own system of property relations. Decollectivization involved much more than the simple introduction, or re-introduction, of capitalist institutions.

CHAPTER 6

LATER YEARS

● ● ●

THE BERNSTEIN ISRAEL RESEARCH PROJECT

It is not clear exactly when Gluckman first met Sidney (Lord) Bernstein (1899–1993) and his brother, Cecil. The Bernsteins were not members of the Mancunian Jewish establishment like the Markses, Sieffs, Sachers or Laskis. As cinema proprietors and film producers, they had moved north from London in the early 1950s to establish Granada, a commercial television franchise for the Manchester region. It is best known as the creator of the long-running soap opera *Coronation Street*. Sidney Bernstein appears to have approached Gluckman in 1959 with a request that he launch a project for the study of immigration into Israel, which had been an independent state for just over a decade. Gluckman and Emrys Peters drew up a plan for the project and an agreement was concluded in 1963 under which the Bernsteins agreed to provide £11,000 a year (about £250,000 a year today) for seven years for the project. With some additional funding from the British Social Science Research fund, it was to run for a further two years until 1971. The plan provided for comparative studies of family and kinship, for studies of the relationships between different ethnic communities in modern enclaves and factories, and for studies of old-established Jewish and non-Jewish communities (this section is largely based on Marx (1975: 131–50) and Shokeid (2004: 387–410)).

Gluckman and Peters recruited ten researchers from Israel, the United Kingdom, the United States and Canada. Emanuel Marx (1927–2022), an Israeli who had completed a Ph.D. in Manchester with Emrys Peters (1916–87) on the Bedouin of Sinai in 1963, was the senior researcher and became the coordinator in Israel. The researchers were trained in Manchester by Gluckman, Peters and Epstein in fieldwork, and all except Marx, who already had a Ph.D., were registered for Manchester Ph.Ds. Gluckman told them to avoid political involvement – his advice was 'Keep your eyes and your ears open and your mouths shut'. The idea was that the research topics would constitute a representative sample of immigrant communities, but the researchers were allowed to choose their own topics and came up with a narrow range of subjects. Four out of ten chose to study cooperative farming villages – *moshavim* on which only 4% of the Israeli population lived – and two chose communal farming villages – *kibbutzim*. Three researchers chose new 'developmental' towns and one chose a workshop for the disabled. In ethnic terms, three of the topics related to Jewish immigrants from North Africa. Moshe Shokeid, for example, chose to study immigrants from the Atlas Mountains of Morocco to a *moshav* in the Negev.

Gluckman was heavily involved in the administration of the project and paid regular visits to researchers in the field in Israel. He was, however, unable to pursue his own interest in immigrants to Israel from South Africa, of which his own family provided an outstanding example. In the view of Moshe Shokeid (born 1936), the researchers met when Gluckman visited Israel, but they never created anything like the solidarity of the RLI fieldworkers. Gluckman was, as always, meticulous in his supervision of the doctoral dissertations written by the researchers and in editing the books that emerged from the project. He wrote forewords for the four books, which were published by Manchester University Press during his lifetime: Shlomo Deshen, *Immigrant Voters in Israel: Parties and Congregations in a Local Election Campaign* (1970); Moshe Shokeid, *The Dual Heritage: Immigrants from the Atlas Mountains in an Israeli Village* (1971); Elaine Baldwin, *Differentiation and Cooperation in an Israeli Veteran Moshav* (1972);

and Myron Joel Aronoff, *Frontier Town: The Politics of Community Building in Israel* (1974). He also completed the supervision of Ph.Ds. by Terence Evens and Don Handelman. According to Shokeid, 'he had never imposed on us any sort of theoretical or ideological orthodoxy'. He appeared to be liberal in his theoretical views: 'It was always the compatibility of data to theory that bothered him'. When Emanuel Marx tried to create a composite picture of Israeli society based on ten years of work by the ten researchers, he found that it was an impossible task because they had not covered the whole ground. There can, however, be no doubt that the Bernstein project did establish social anthropology in Israel and provided a continuing link with Manchester.

Gluckman was never a Zionist, but he did establish a strong link with Israel in the 1960s. Like many Jews in the diaspora, he was, with Mary, greatly disturbed by the Six-Day War in 1967. Two of their three sons volunteered for service in Israel and he and Mary both sought to volunteer, though they were too old for service. According to David Boswell, the research in Israel may have contributed to tension in the department. He recalled a residential conference presided over by Gluckman at John Ruskin's house, Brantwood, near Coniston Water in the Lake District, in circa 1968. Emanuel Marx, the senior researcher on the Bernstein project, who, according to Boswell, had a role in the occupied Sinai Peninsula after the Six-Day War, gave a paper on an agricultural development scheme for Palestinians 'in which he took a poor view either of their commitment or capability'. In the discussion of the paper, Boswell, anticipating later Israel-apartheid debates, observed that 'if we had been discussing a similar situation in Southern Rhodesia for resettled Africans on poor land after the sequestration of their original lands by White farmers on government subsidies, we would be assessing their situation on quite different terms'. Kingsley Garbett, who had recently returned from Southern Rhodesia after UDI (Southern Rhodesia's Unilateral Declaration of Independence in 1965), agreed with Boswell and provided some examples. Gluckman 'promptly exploded off his chair, raising his arms in the air, condemning this outright, [exclaiming] "How dare you say that", and denying any similarity... [he] effectively closed the session's discussion down forthwith'. Boswell does not, however, think that this incident had an adverse effect on his relationship with Gluckman (David Boswell, interview and email, 7 July 2022).

SOCIAL ANTHROPOLOGY VERSUS SOCIOLOGY

It was unfortunate that the last decade of Gluckman's life was overshadowed by failing health and tensions within the joint Department of Social Anthropology and Sociology, which culminated in a formal split in 1971. He had a heart attack in 1968 and an operation for prostate cancer in 1969. The tension became apparent soon after Peter Worsley's appointment to the Professorship of Sociology in 1964. Jack Simons, who had a Simon Fellowship from 1965 to 1967, said that that he had found the tension between Gluckman and Worsley, who had been Gluckman's student and his candidate for the post, distressing, and David Boswell also felt it (Jack Simons and David Boswell, conversation and interview, 2022). Ronnie Frankenberg traced the tension in the Manchester department, and the tensions between the disciplines of social anthropology and sociology further back, to 1956, and the two crises involving the Soviet invasion of Hungary and the joint Anglo-French, and Israeli, Suez Campaign (Frankenberg 1989: 165). The former prompted many members, including Victor and Edith Turner, to resign from the Communist Party of Great Britain (CPGB), and the latter increased tension between supporters and opponents of Zionism and the State of Israel. Other commentators, including Worsley, linked this tension to the report of the Robins Commission on higher education in 1963, the opening of many new universities with sociology (but not social anthropology) departments and the great expansion in student numbers. According to Worsley, there was an influx of students to sociology in Manchester, which was part of a worldwide rise in the popularity of the subject. This had 'a fateful consequence' for a social anthropology department that had an international reputation, but which was now threatened by the rise of sociology. In his view, the only solution was to separate the departments.

> Max, naturally, fought tooth and nail to stop this happening, since it might have reduced anthropology to a rump. I argued that anthropology would have to move away from its traditional focus upon 'tribal' societies and begin to tackle problems of development in the Third World, particularly new forms of rural organization and urban life. If it didn't the subject would simply wither away. This naturally infuriated Max and the anthropologists, and when I followed this up by giving a paper at the Evian World Congress of Sociology [in 1966] entitled 'The End of Anthropology?', his fury knew no bounds. (Worsley 2008: 124)

In his paper Worsley had suggested that if anthropology continued to focus on 'primitive peoples', it would 'inexorably die out with its subject matter'. He had the grace to add in a footnote to this passage of his memoir: 'I was wrong – it didn't die at all.'

Worsley's paper was, however, only the first salvo in a round of critical attacks on British social anthropology in the context of decolonization and the end of empire. They included 'Anthropology and Imperialism' (1967) by Kathleen Gough (1925–90) and 'The Crisis of British Anthropology' by Jairus Banaji (born 1947), which described British anthropology as 'stagnating in theory [and] threatened as a practice'. It concluded with a resounding call for 'research into the genocidal practices of imperialism and a truly scientific comprehension of the social and cultural ensembles it has destroyed' (Banaji 1970). In one of his last public interventions, a response to a special issue of *The Times Literary Supplement* on social anthropology (6 July 1973), which included articles by Evans-Pritchard, Leach and Douglas, Gluckman referred to a widespread belief in a 'mysterious underlying adherence of all anthropologists to colonialist domination' and he said that social anthropology was 'too complex to be explained simply as a product of colonialism' (Gluckman 1973b: 905).

Gluckman must also have been aware that social anthropology had come under a cloud of suspicion in newly independent African states, including Zambia, where it was seen by many as the handmaid of colonialism. Few, if any, new universities in independent Africa had social anthropology departments. Bernard (Ben) Magubane (1930–2013), a South African sociologist with an American university postgraduate education, taught in the sociology department at the new (1966) University of Zambia with Ronnie Frankenberg and Jack Simons in 1967–69. He joined the African National Congress (ANC) in exile in Lusaka and returned to the United States, where he became a founder of the American Anti-Apartheid Movement. He published an article in *Current Anthropology* in 1971, which, though not mentioning Gluckman by name, was critical of social anthropology in general and of the Copperbelt research of Epstein and Mitchell in particular. Magubane took issue with what he saw as their use of phenomena such as diet and clothing as indices of 'civilization' or 'Westernization'. The kernel of his argument came in the concluding paragraph of his article:

> My criticism of Epstein and Mitchell must not be interpreted as saying that they were tools of colonialists or imperialists, but only that their interpretation of phenomena was at times extremely superficial and at best ethnocentric. Their analyses failed to overcome their European perspective. As men who basically accepted the 'civilizing mission' of imperialism, their analyses rationalized and attempted to improve the imperial system. (Magubane 1971: 431)

The editors of *Current Anthropology* provided space for replies from Epstein and Mitchell, who both accused Magubane of setting them up as 'straw men'; for comments from many other scholars including Philip Mayer (1910–95) and Ezekiel Mphahlele (1919–2008); and for a closing reply from Magubane. His arguments, for all that they could be shown by his targets to be misinformed or unfair, were widely accepted as an accurate characterization of colonial social anthropology by Black scholars and students in Southern Africa in the 1970s. With the passage of time, these views were moderated. At a conference held at the Institute of Social Research in Lusaka in 1989 to commemorate the fiftieth anniversary of the founding of the RLI, Professor Mubanga Kashoki (born 1938), a former director of the institute and the then Vice-Chancellor of the Copperbelt University, pointed out that these critics had often taken a simplistic view, ignoring the frequent conflicts between social anthropologists and the colonial government. He also stressed the advantages of the long-term commitment to fieldwork of social anthropologists, when compared with the contemporary fashion for short-term consultancies (Mubanga Kashoki, 'The Role of Universities in Social Science Research', seminar paper, Lusaka, 1989, quoted in Colson 1992).

As if the assault on social anthropology in British and African universities was not enough, Gluckman also had to contend, as did many other senior academics, including other one-time radicals, with the wave of student radicalism that swept through the universities, including Manchester, in 1968–69. Peter Worsley may not have been the most impartial observer, though he displayed no animosity towards Gluckman, but his views of Gluckman's response are backed up by those of others:

Very sadly, one of the people most hostile to the students was Max Gluckman. He had been very bitter about the revelations in the Soviet Union (feeling, I think, that he had been made a fool of) and his South African upbringing had imbued him with a postcolonial reverence for British academia, especially Oxbridge . . . He did not lose his anticolonialism or his social egalitarianism, but these events took him quite a way on the all too familiar, tiresome journey from leftwinger to reactionary. At the height of the student protests, he had to be virtually physically restrained when militant students tried to prevent him and anyone else going through the door of the senate they were picketing. (Worsley 2008: 159)

In his editorial introduction to *Profiles of Change*, the third volume of *Colonialism in Africa, 1870–1960*, a series edited by Lewis Gann and Peter Duignan, Victor Turner reflected in 1971 on the anthropologists' transition from 'socialist' to 'reactionary':

> It used to be argued by officials of the *ancien régime* that anthropologists, immersed as they were in the specificities of African life, came to accept the structural perspective of their informants, became their spokesmen, and by their words and works impeded the efforts of district and provincial administrators to govern efficiently. Some were even accused by white settlers and European civil servants of being 'Reds', 'socialists' and 'anarchists'. It is now asseverated by African leaders and administrators, down to the district level, that anthropologists before independence were 'apologists of colonialism' and subtle agents of colonial supremacy who studied African customs merely to provide the dominant white minority with information damaging to native interests but normally opaque to white investigation. (Turner 1971: 1)

In his own contribution to this volume, 'Tribalism, and Urbanism in South and Central Africa', Gluckman undertook 'to make some predictions or guesses about future developments'. He acknowledged that the subject was 'a highly emotive one' and that some of his interpretations of the facts might lead to 'varying allegations about my political attitudes and motives'. He continued: 'I therefore affirm these at the start. I have been, in feeling and in action, on the side of the Africans in their struggle against apartheid, and in their striving for independence elsewhere in Africa.' Nevertheless, he insisted that:

> the facts ... show that over a fair run of time the Republic of South Africa is likely to manifest considerable internal stability ... and the sharp divisions between its colour-groups are unlikely to lead to revolution unless there is international intervention. On the other hand, independent Afri-

can states are unlikely to show that stability, but are likely to be more subject to internal coups and crowd violence. I come to these conclusions despite my political wishes. (Gluckman 1971b: 127)

Gluckman's views on the lack of revolutionary prospects in South Africa reflected the views that he had expressed in the 'Analysis' over thirty years previously and his later views on conflict and cohesion. They may also have reflected a later debate in the journal *Africa South* in 1958 between his friends Julius Lewin and Jack Simons on the theme of 'No Revolution Around The Corner', in which Lewin took Gluckman's position and Simons was more optimistic about the prospects for change in South Africa (Macmillan 2016: 62–65). As late as 1988, Harold Wolpe (1926–96), a South African radical, seemed to reflect Gluckman and the 'Analysis' when he wrote in *Race, Class and the Apartheid State* that 'even if the regime cannot tilt the balance in its own favour, a situation of unstable equilibrium may be maintained over a long period of time' (Wolpe 1988: 110).

Gluckman died in 1975 at the very moment that Chief Gatsha Buthelezi (1928–2023), son of his old acquaintance Chief Mathole, was beginning to emerge as the leader of Inkhata, a new political party, derived from the earlier cultural movement, which claimed an association with the banned ANC. Gluckman did not visit South Africa between 1947 and his death, but he would not have been entirely surprised at Buthelezi and Inkhata's political oscillation over the next twenty years between a wider African nationalism and a narrower Zulu ethnic chauvinism (Macmillan 1995: 64).

AMONG THE 'GREAT AND THE GOOD'

By the 1960s, Gluckman had become a recognized member of the British and international academic establishments. He was a member of the council of the International African Institute (1956–65), consultative director (1966–74) and vice-chairman

(1974). He was honorary secretary of the Association of Social Anthropologists of the British Commonwealth (1951–57) and was also chairman (1962–66). He was elected to a fellowship of the British Academy (FBA) in 1968 and to a foreign honorary membership of the American Academy of Arts and Sciences in 1970. He was made an honorary D.Soc.Sci. at the Free University of Brussels in 1965. He was invited to give the Frazer Lecture at the University of Glasgow in 1952; the Munro Lectures at the University of Edinburgh in 1958 and 1960; the Storrs Lectures at Yale in 1963; the Marett Lectures – he spoke on 'Moral Crises: Magical and Secular Solutions' – at Exeter College, Oxford in 1964 and 1965; and the Radcliffe-Brown Lecture at the British Academy in 1974. He was awarded the Wellcome and Rivers Medals by the Royal Anthropological Institute. He held visiting lectureships at a dozen universities, including the Hebrew University of Jerusalem and Yale. He was also a member of the social studies subcommittee of the University Grants Committee (1966–70) and of the advisory committee of the Sports Council (1974), an appointment that gave him great pleasure (Fortes 2004).

Gluckman retired from his Manchester University chair at the age of sixty on 31 August 1971, at the same time as the final split between the Social Anthropology and Sociology Departments took place. He was then appointed to a Nuffield research professorship at Manchester with a seven-year term from 1 September 1971.[1] He accepted a Lady Davis visiting professorship at the Hebrew University of Jerusalem for 1974–75 and he died there, following a heart attack, on 13 April 1975, at the age of sixty-four. He left his body to medical science. Following his death, Mary Gluckman spent over two years as a senior Voluntary Service Overseas (VSO) volunteer in Sierra Leone and died in England in 1990 at the age of seventy-three. With Max she was an energetic walker, and she is commemorated by a plaque in Hyning Scout Wood, in Lancashire, a wood that is maintained by the Woodland Trust.

Max Gluckman died too soon. His exact agemate, Hilda Kuper, lived another seventeen years and died at the age of eighty-one in Los Angeles in 1992. Elizabeth Colson, who was only six years his junior, lived for another forty-one years and died in Monze, Zambia, at the age of ninety-nine in 2016.

NOTE

1. Information by courtesy of James Peters, university archivist, University of Manchester, 27 September 2022.

CONCLUSION

* * *

PERSONALITY

The words and phrases most frequently used to describe Max Gluckman's personality are charismatic, larger-than-life, brilliant, generous and argumentative. On the positive side, Max was by all accounts a devoted husband to Mary for nearly forty years and a good father to three sons. He was a dedicated teacher and mentor, who spent long hours meticulously editing the theses and books of his students and colleagues. He also wrote generous references for them and did his best to promote their careers. He and Mary were unfailingly hospitable in their Cheadle Hume home. Phyllis Deane, who was close to him in 1946–47, described Max as 'a charismatic person who had an inspiring influence'. She said that she did not know anyone who had worked with him who did not share such positive views of him (Phyllis Deane, interview, 1993). On the negative side, one well-informed source said that he had a highly developed persecution complex, was intolerant of any criticism, was incapable of treating juniors as equals and was unwilling to allow anyone else to be the centre of attention. The source added that he was also 'a formidable bully'. In the same vein, though more humorously, Peter Worsley noted that 'Max was, as everyone recognised, what passes for the stereotype of the authoritarian African chief'. And commenting on his practice of enrolling postgraduate students in domestic work parties, he noted that '[h]e was also an upper-class white South

African, used to having servants to do what he wanted, including working in his garden' (Worsley 2008: 75).

It would be possible to assemble a multitude of similarly contrasting quotations about Gluckman. In 1995, Lewis Gann provided a convincing character sketch of Gluckman as he appeared to a German-Jewish refugee, and a self-confessedly conservative observer, in Manchester in 1952–54. He described him as 'above all . . . a kind and generous friend, cheerful and open-minded, a man who loved intellectual controversy'. He stressed his generosity, his openness to debate and his lack of religious, ethnic or even political prejudice:

> I am sure that Gluckman was agnostic in religion. Politically he belonged to the 'soft left' – shaped by the Spanish Civil War and the tradition of the Popular Front. I remember arguing with him about the Soviet Union. He insisted that the Soviet Union – unlike a capitalist state – was not subject to economic crises. I pleaded that the Soviets had plunged the country into a permanent crisis. But he did not see it my way. His wife was once a communist. I am sure he was never a communist. He was far too loyal to the British Empire. I am sure that Gluckman was never a Zionist. Personally, I was always struck by his kindness, his intellectual and personal generosity, his willingness to argue. (In fact, he enjoyed arguing with me, even though I was a conservative even at that time.) Gluckman was also unusual among leftists in that he liked the USA, liked Americans, thought the US was 'a great country' – despite its capitalistic flaws. He was also one of the few British academics who took US scholarship seriously. When I was in Manchester, 1952–4, he invited people such as Edward Shils and George Homans to lecture at the Department of Anthropology. Gluckman was a man totally devoid of ethnic prejudice. He had no hostility toward Germans (common among Jewish people at that time). He was very kind also to my German Gentile wife whom I married after the Second World War. (Macmillan papers: Lewis Gann to Hugh Macmillan,

17 April 1995, and memorandum for Hugh Macmillan on
Gluckman, postmarked 24 April 1995)

Intellectual and personal generosity, as the Lozi of Katongo dis-
cerned, and acknowledged, with the *Makapweka* nickname in
the early 1940s, do seem to have been his outstanding charac-
teristics. It is noticeable in his always punctilious acknowledgement of helpers, useful ideas and sources. But this is sometimes
difficult to reconcile with his propensity for long-running battles
with fellow academics. Elizabeth Colson, who knew him as well
as anyone did, said that 'Max loved a good feud'. She also said:
'We always said, and Max agreed, that all his questions were political ones' (author's recollections and Macmillan papers: Colson to Macmillan, 27 June 2000). She had in mind his feud with
Edmund Leach, but it would be possible to cite many more. Suitably, for a man who gave a frequently quoted broadcast entitled
'The Peace in the Feud' (Gluckman 1956: 1–26), these were not
usually conducted in such a way as to produce lasting bitterness
or animosity. As Raymond Firth noted in his British Academy
memoir: 'He may have had critics, but he had no enemies' (Firth
1975: 496).

It may also be the case that these feuds were often conducted
with relish on both sides. Nearly a decade after Gluckman's death,
Edmund Leach wrote, in an apparently antisemitic and definitely
snobbish article entitled 'Glimpses of the Unmentionable in the
History of British Social Anthropology', that he had taken 'an
instant dislike' to Gluckman when he first encountered him at
Radcliffe-Brown's seminar in Oxford in 1938–39. He said that he
would in the past have described him as 'an uncivilized and fun-
damentally uneducated egocentric whose attempts at generaliza-
tion were of quite puerile incompetence'. He went on to explain
that 'it was a radical difference of social background rather than
any fundamental disagreement regarding social theory that lay
at the root of our mutual antipathy'. Acknowledging that 'such
arrogance and prejudice on my part reflects no credit on me', he
stressed that he had not changed his views. He defended his right
to hold and publish such views with the recommendation that:

'Unless we pay much closer attention than has been customary to the personal background of the authors of anthropological works, we shall miss out on what these texts are capable of telling us about the history of anthropology' (Leach 1984: 1–22).

It would be tedious in the extreme to list the names of people with whom Gluckman had feuds or major fallings-out. He himself attributed violent fits of temper in his RLI days to duodenal ulcers (Mitchell papers: Gluckman to Mitchell, 5 November 1951). He spent many years under analysis and, by some accounts, this may have helped to calm him down. At the same time, some of his rows may have been justified. He had a major break with Evans-Pritchard in 1955 when he heard that 'E.P.' was campaigning to stop Epstein's appointment to the directorship of the RLI and was spreading the malicious (and unfounded) rumour that he was a card-carrying member of the Communist Party (Mitchell papers: Gluckman to Mitchell, 15 July 1955). There is no doubt that 'E.P.', a rabid anti-communist with self-confessed antisemitic tendencies, was guilty as charged. The storm does, however, seem to have blown over and they were reconciled by the early 1960s. Gluckman dedicated his last edited collection, *The Allocation of Responsibility*, to 'E.P.'. He described the book, all but one of whose eight contributors had been a member of his department, as a tribute to 'E.P.' from Manchester (Gluckman 1972b: ix).

Whether or not Gluckman had a persecution complex, he was always hypersensitive, and in the last few years of his life, when he was physically unwell, he showed increasing signs of what Clyde Mitchell called 'irrational insecurity'. Correspondence with Emrys Peters in 1970–1 indicates that he was reluctant to cede control of the department as he moved towards a research professorship and quick to accuse Peters of abuse (Gordon 2018: 382–83; and extracts of Gluckman–Peters correspondence courtesy of Sarah Walpole of the RAI). At much the same time, he seemed to want to pick a fight with Mitchell about the origins of network theory. He also became involved in a fight by correspondence with Victor Turner, one of his oldest and closest friends, who had, unfairly, suggested in the introduction to *The Ritual*

Process (1969) that he had received no encouragement from the RLI – in other words, Gluckman, Colson and Mitchell – for the pursuit of his interest in ritual. He had also suggested that the RLI was responding to pressure from the colonial government in directing its researchers, including himself, towards the collection of 'hard-nosed data' on labour migration and industrialization. The argument ended with a kind of reconciliation, but the correspondence is painful to read (Mitchell to Raymond Firth, 22 October 1975, quoted in Gordon 2018: 382–83; Werbner 2020: 234–41).

LEGACY

This book is a contribution to a series on 'Anthropology's Ancestors'. It would not be difficult to place Gluckman in a social anthropological genealogy with Malinowski and Radcliffe-Brown as his parents, and Emile Durkheim, Sigmund Freud, Sir Henry Maine and Karl Marx, as, in alphabetical order, his multidisciplinary grandparents and great-grandparents. Winifred Hoernlé might be a little difficult to place, but she would, presumably, also be a parent. Edward Evans-Pritchard, Raymond Firth, Meyer Fortes, Edmund Leach, Audrey Richards and Isaac Schapera, together with Godfrey and Monica Wilson, would be his elder siblings, Hilda Kuper his agemate and twin, and Mary Douglas a younger sibling. His descendants may be more difficult to identify and he could not claim to be the sole intellectual progenitor of any of them. Shortly before his death, he claimed that eleven out of twelve people who had served as full-time researchers at the RLI had become professors in various parts of the world from California to Australia. They included Elizabeth Colson, Clyde Mitchell, John Barnes, Victor Turner, Bill Epstein, Ian Cunnison and William Watson, all of whom must have their own intellectual descendants. Two of his postgraduate students at Manchester, Ronnie Frankenberg and Peter Worsley, had been prevented from joining the RLI, but had already by the time of his death gone on to become professors. Younger members of their generation included Bruce Kapferer and Richard Werbner, who in his book *Anthropology after Gluckman: The Manchester School, Colonial and Postcolonial Transformations* (2020) has identified some of the next generation of Gluckman's intellectual descendants.

In his essay on the anthropologists of 'Britain and the Commonwealth', Fredrik Barth noted that the retirement of Firth, Evans-Pritchard, Fortes and Gluckman had closed a chapter in the history of British anthropology. He observed that: 'Their successors, however gifted and productive, could never recreate the conditions of authority and intellectual leadership that had once prevailed' (Barth 2005: 53).

Gluckman's varied legacy, institutionally through the RLI and Manchester, and intellectually through fieldwork in Zululand and Barotseland, has been described in this book. He believed that he was 'entitled to describe himself as the author of pioneering studies in legal anthropology' and he saw this as his greatest achievement (Gluckman 1973b: 905). It is hard, however, to resist the conclusion that it was his 'Analysis' of a day spent with many others, both Black and white, at 'the Bridge' over the Malungwana Drift in Zululand in January 1938, that had the greatest and most enduring impact. Writing about named people in real time in a named place, and about real events in a multi-ethnic community, Max Gluckman helped to shatter the 'bounded tribe', to dissolve the 'ethnographic present' and to begin the process of bringing British (and South African) social anthropology into the modern world.

SELECTED WORKS BY MAX GLUCKMAN

●　●　●

1935. 'Zulu Women in Hoe Culture Ritual'. *Bantu Studies* 9(3): 255–72.

1936. 'The Realm of the Supernatural among the South-Eastern Bantu', D.Phil. dissertation. Oxford: University of Oxford.

1940. 'The Kingdom of the Zulu of South Africa', in M. Fortes and E. Evans-Pritchard (eds), *African Political Systems*. London: Oxford University Press, 25–55.

1943. *Administrative Organization of the Barotse Native Authorities*. Livingstone: RLI Communications 1.

1944a. 'Obituary, Godfrey Baldwin Wilson'. *Human Problems in British Central Africa* 1: 1–3.

1944b. 'The Difficulties, Achievements and Limitations of Social Anthropology'. *Human Problems in British Central Africa* 1: 23–45.

1945a. 'Zambesi River Kingdom'. *Libertas* 5(8): 20–39.

1945b. 'Seven-Year Research Plan of the Rhodes-Livingstone Institute of Social Studies in British Central Africa'. *Human Problems in British Central Africa* 4: 1–32.

1946. 'Human Laboratory across the Zambesi'. *Libertas* 6(4): 38–49.

1948. 'Director's Report to the Trustees of the Work of the Years, 1944–5–6'. *Human Problems in British Central Africa* 6: 64–79.

1949. *Malinowski's Sociological Theories*. Livingstone: RLI.

1951. 'The Lozi of Barotseland in North-Western Rhodesia', in Elizabeth Colson and Max Gluckman (eds), *Seven Tribes of British Central Africa*. London: Oxford University Press for RLI, 1–93.

1954. *Rituals of Rebellion in South-East Africa*. Manchester: Manchester University Press.

1956. *Custom and Conflict in Africa*. Oxford: Basil Blackwell.

1958. *Analysis of a Social Situation in Modern Zululand.* Manchester: Manchester University Press (first published in three parts in *Bantu/African Studies*, 1940, 1942).

1960. 'Rise of a Zulu Empire'. *Scientific American* 202: 157–69.

(ed.). 1962. *Essays on the Ritual of Social Relations.* Manchester: Manchester University Press.

1963. *Ritual and Rebellion in Tribal Africa.* Manchester: Manchester University Press.

1965. *Politics, Law and Ritual in Tribal Society.* Oxford: Basil Blackwell.

1968a [1941]. *Economy of the Central Barotse Plain.* Manchester: Manchester University Press.

1968b [1943]. *Essays on Lozi Land and Royal Property.* Manchester: Manchester University Press, 1968.

1969. 'Property Rights and Status in African Traditional Law', in Max Gluckman (ed.), *Ideas and Procedures in African Customary Law.* Oxford: Oxford University Press, 252–65.

1971a. 'The Tribal Area in South and Central Africa', in Leo Kuper and M.G. Smith (eds) *Pluralism in Africa.* Berkeley: University of California Press, 373–409.

1971b. 'Tribalism, Ruralism and Urbanism in South and Central Africa', in Victor Turner, (ed.), *Colonialism in Africa. Volume 3. Profiles of Change: African Society and Colonial Rule.* Cambridge: Cambridge University Press, 127–166.

1972a. *The Ideas in Barotse Jurisprudence*, 2nd edn. Manchester: Manchester University Press.

(ed.). 1972b. *The Allocation of Responsibility.* Manchester: Manchester University Press.

1973a. *The Judicial Process among the Barotse*, 2nd edn. Manchester: Manchester University Press.

1973b. 'Letter to the Editor'. *Times Literary Supplement*, 3 August: 905.

1974. 'The Individual in a Social Framework: The Rise of King Shaka'. *Journal of African Studies* 1(2): 113–44.

1975. 'Anthropology and Apartheid: The Work of South African Anthropologists', in M. Fortes and S. Patterson (eds), *Studies in African Social Anthropology.* London: Academic Press, 21–40.

2014. 'Conflict and Cohesion in Zululand: An Historical Study in Social Organization'. *History in Africa* 14(1): 183–94.

REFERENCES

• • •

ARCHIVES

Cambridge. Emmanuel College: Gluckman papers.
Dorchester on Thames, Wallingford, Oxfordshire: Hugh Macmillan papers.
London. RAI: Gluckman papers.
London. SOAS: Movement for Colonial Freedom papers; Fox-Pitt papers.
Lusaka. Zambia National Archives: RLI files.
Oxford. Bodleian Library: Africa Bureau papers.
Oxford. Bodleian Library: J.C. Mitchell papers.
Oxford. Bodleian Library: Sir Roy Welensky papers.
Pretoria. National Archives, NTS files.

AUTHOR'S INTERVIEWS

Apthorpe, Raymond. London, 29 September 2022.
Boswell, David. Oxford, 7 July 2022.
Deane, Phyllis. Cambridge, 10 February 1993.
Kuper, Hilda, with Leo Kuper. Los Angeles, 14 April 1983.

ONLINE INTERVIEWS

Colson, Elizabeth, 2002. 'Anthropology and a Lifetime of Observation: Oral History Transcript, 2002'. Retrieved 18 August 2023 from https://www.ebooksread.com/authors-eng/elizabeth-colson/anthropology-and-a-lifetime-of-observation--oral-history-transcript--2002-hci/page-

12-anthropology-and-a-lifetime-of-observation--oral-history-tran
script--2002-hci.shtml.

———. 2006. Interview with Alan MacFarlane and talk by Elizabeth Colson,
April [video file]. Retrieved 18 August 2023 from http://www.dspace
.cam.ac.uk/handle/1810/183616.

BOOKS, ARTICLES AND DISSERTATIONS

Allan, William, Max Gluckman, D.U Peters and Colin G. Trapnell. 1948.
*Land Holding and Land Usage among the Plateau Tonga of Mazabuka
District: A Reconnaissance Survey, 1945.* Livingstone: RLI, 1948 (2nd edn,
Manchester: Manchester University Press, 1968).

Banaji, Jairus. 1970. 'The Crisis of British Anthropology'. *New Left Review*
64 (November/December). Retrieved 5 September 2023 from https://
newleftreview.org/issues/i64/articles/jairus-banaji-the-crisis-of-brit
ish-anthropology.

Bank, Andrew. 2016. *Pioneers of the Field: South Africa's Women Anthropologists.* Cambridge: Cambridge University Press.

Barnes, John. 2007. *Humping My Drum: A Memoir.* Print-on-demand, www
.lulu.com.

Barth, Fredrik. 2005. 'Britain and the Commonwealth', in F. Barth, A. Gin-
grich, R. Parkin and S. Silverman, *One Discipline, Four Ways: British,
German, French and American Anthropology.* Chicago: University of
Chicago Press, 3–60.

Bloch, Maurice. 1983. *Marxism and Anthropology.* Oxford: Oxford University Press.

Bošković, Aleksandar, and Günther Schlee (eds). 2022. *African Political Systems Revisited.* Oxford: Berghahn Books.

Brown, Richard. 1979. 'Passages in the Life of a White Anthropologist: Max
Gluckman in Northern Rhodesia'. *Journal of African History* 20: 525–40.

Cannadine, David. 1983. 'The Context, Performance and Meaning of Ritual:
The British Monarchy and the "Invention of Tradition" c. 1820–1977', in
Eric Hobsbawm and Terence Ranger (eds), *The Invention of Tradition.*
Cambridge: Cambridge University Press, 101–64.

Chanock, Martin. 1985. *Law, Custom and Social Order: The Colonial Experience in Malawi and Zambia.* Cambridge: Cambridge University Press.

Clarence-Smith, W.G. 1979. 'Slaves, Commoners and Landlords in Bulozi,
c. 1875–1906'. *Journal of African History* 20(2): 219–34.

Clay, Geoffrey F. 1945. *Memorandum on Post War Development Planning in
Northern Rhodesia.* Lusaka: Government Printer.

Cocks, Paul. 2001. 'Max Gluckman and the Critique of Segregation in South African Anthropology, 1921–40'. *Journal of Southern African Studies* 27(4): 729–56.

Colson, Elizabeth. 1977a. 'The Institute under Max Gluckman, 1942–7'. *African Social Research* 24: 285–95.

———. 1977b. 'From Livingstone to Lusaka, 1948–51'. *African Social Research* 24: 297–307.

———. 'Max Gluckman and the Study of Divorce', in P.H. Gulliver (ed.), *Cross-Examinations: Essays in Memory of Max Gluckman*. Leiden: Brill, 15–28.

———. 1992. 'The Relevance of Irrelevant Studies: The Future of Anthropology in Development Research'. *Zambia Journal of History* 5: 1–13.

———. 2008. 'Defining "The Manchester School of Anthropology"'. Review of T.M.S Elvers and Don Handelman, *The Manchester School: Practice and Ethnographic Praxis in Anthropology. Current Anthropology* 49: 335–37.

Colson, Elizabeth, and Max Gluckman (eds). 1951. *Seven Tribes of British Central Africa*. London: Oxford University Press for RLI.

Davidson, Basil. 1992. *The Black Man's Burden*. London: James Currey.

Douglas, Mary. 1959. 'Review of Watson, (ed.) *Tribal Cohesion in a Money Economy'. Man* 59: 168.

Epstein, A.L. 1965. *The Craft of Social Anthropology*. London: Tavistock Press.

Eriksen, T.H. 2013. *Fredrik Barth: An Intellectual Biography*. London: Pluto Press.

Evans-Pritchard, Edward E. 1937. *Witchcraft, Oracles, and Magic among the Azande*. Oxford: Oxford University Press.

Evens, T., and D. Handyman (eds). 2006. *The Manchester School: Practice and Ethnographic Praxis in Anthropology*. New York: Berghahn Books.

Fallers, Lloyd. 1959. 'Review of Gluckman, *Analysis of a Social Situation in Modern Zululand'. American Anthropologist* 61(6): 1122.

Firth, Raymond. 1975. 'Max Gluckman, 1911–75'. *Proceedings of the British Academy* 61: 479–96.

Foreman, P. 2014. 'Horizons of Modernity: British Anthropology and the End of Empire', Ph.D. dissertation. Berkeley: University of California.

Fortes, Meyer, and Edward Evans-Pritchard (eds). 1940. *African Political Systems*. London: Oxford University Press.

Fortes, Meyer. 2004. 'Gluckman, (Herman) Max (1911–75)', in *Oxford Dictionary of National Biography*. Oxford: Oxford University Press, published in print and online.

Frank, Katherine. 2002. *The Life of Indira Nehru Gandhi*. London: Harper Collins.

Frankenberg, Ronald. 1989 [1957]. 'Village on the Border: A Text Revisited. 1989', in *A Village on the Border: A Social Study of Religion, Politics and Football in a North Wales Community*. Long Grove, IL: Waveland Press, Inc., 169–93.

———. 2005. 'A Bridge over Troubled Waters, or What a Difference a Day Makes: From the Drama of Production to the Production of Drama'. *Social Analysis: The International Journal of Anthropology* 49(3): 166–94.

———. 2006. 'Foreword', in Edith Turner, *Heart of Lightness*. Oxford: Berghahn Books, xi–xxvi.

Gann, Lewis H. 1993. 'Ex Africa: An Africanist's Intellectual Autobiography'. *Journal of Modern African Studies* 31(3): 477–98.

Gluckman, Max.1935. 'Zulu Women in Hoe Culture Ritual'. *Bantu Studies* 9(3): 255–72.

———. 1936. 'The Realm of the Supernatural among the South-Eastern Bantu', D.Phil. dissertation. Oxford: University of Oxford.

———. 1940. 'The Kingdom of the Zulu of South Africa', in M. Fortes and E. Evans-Pritchard (eds), *African Political Systems*. London: Oxford University Press, 25–55.

———. 1943. *Administrative Organization of the Barotse Native Authorities*. Livingstone: RLI Communications 1.

———. 1944a. 'Obituary, Godfrey Baldwin Wilson'. *Human Problems in British Central Africa* 1: 1–3.

———. 1944b. 'The Difficulties, Achievements and Limitations of Social Anthropology'. *Human Problems in British Central Africa* 1: 23–45.

———. 1945a. 'Zambesi River Kingdom'. *Libertas* 5(8): 20–39.

———. 1945b. 'Seven-Year Research Plan of the Rhodes-Livingstone Institute of Social Studies in British Central Africa'. *Human Problems in British Central Africa* 4: 1–32.

———. 1946. 'Human Laboratory across the Zambesi'. *Libertas* 6(4): 38–49.

———. 1948. 'Director's Report to the Trustees of the Work of the Years, 1944-5-6'. *Human Problems in British Central Africa* 6: 64–79.

———. 1949. *Malinowski's Sociological Theories*. Livingstone: RLI.

———. 1951. 'The Lozi of Barotseland in North-Western Rhodesia', in Elizabeth Colson and Max Gluckman (eds), *Seven Tribes of British Central Africa*. London: Oxford University Press for RLI, 1–93.

———. 1954. *Rituals of Rebellion in South-East Africa*. Manchester: Manchester University Press.

———. 1956. *Custom and Conflict in Africa*. Oxford: Basil Blackwell.

———. 1958. *Analysis of a Social Situation in Modern Zululand*. Manchester: Manchester University Press (first published in three parts in *Bantu/African Studies*, 1940, 1942).

———. 1960. 'Rise of a Zulu Empire'. *Scientific American* 202: 157–69.

———. (ed.). 1962. *Essays on the Ritual of Social Relations*. Manchester: Manchester University Press.

———. 1963. *Ritual and Rebellion in Tribal Africa*. Manchester: Manchester University Press.

———. 1965. *Politics, Law and Ritual in Tribal Society*. Oxford: Basil Blackwell.

———. 1968a [1941]. *Economy of the Central Barotse Plain*. Manchester: Manchester University Press.

———. 1968b [1943]. *Essays on Lozi Land and Royal Property*. Manchester: Manchester University Press, 1968.

———. 1969. 'Property Rights and Status in African Traditional Law', in Max Gluckman (ed.), *Ideas and Procedures in African Customary Law*. Oxford: Oxford University Press, 252–65.

———. 1971a. 'The Tribal Area in South and Central Africa', in Leo Kuper and M.G. Smith (eds) *Pluralism in Africa*. Berkeley: University of California Press, 373–409.

———. 1971b. 'Tribalism, Ruralism and Urbanism in South and Central Africa', in Victor Turner, (ed.), *Colonialism in Africa. Volume 3. Profiles of Change: African Society and Colonial Rule*. Cambridge: Cambridge University Press, 127–166.

———. 1972a. *The Ideas in Barotse Jurisprudence*, 2nd edn. Manchester: Manchester University Press.

———. (ed.). 1972b. *The Allocation of Responsibility*. Manchester: Manchester University Press.

———. 1973a. *The Judicial Process among the Barotse*, 2nd edn. Manchester: Manchester University Press.

———. 1973b. 'Letter to the Editor'. *Times Literary Supplement*, 3 August: 905.

———. 1974. 'The Individual in a Social Framework: The Rise of King Shaka'. *Journal of African Studies* 1(2): 113–44.

———. 1975. 'Anthropology and Apartheid: The Work of South African Anthropologists', in M. Fortes and S. Patterson (eds), *Studies in African Social Anthropology*. London: Academic Press, 21–40.

———. 2014. 'Conflict and Cohesion in Zululand: An Historical Study in Social Organization'. *History in Africa* 14(1): 183–94.

Gordon, Robert. 2018. *The Enigma of Max Gluckman: The Ethnographic Life of a 'Lucky Man' in Africa*. Lincoln, NE: University of Nebraska Press.

Gough, Kathleen. 1968. 'Anthropology and Imperialism'. *Monthly Review* 19: 12–47.

Gray, Geoffrey. 2019. '"In My File, I Am Two Different People": Max Gluckman and A.L. Epstein, the Australian National University, and Australian

Security Intelligence Organisation, 1958–60'. *Cold War History* 20(1): 1–18.

Gulliver, Philip H. (ed.). 1978. *Cross-Examinations: Essays in Memory of Max Gluckman*. Leiden: Brill.

Hann, Chris. 2022. 'Economy and Ethics in the Cosmic Process'. *Journal of the Royal Anthropological Institute* 28(1): 5–29.

Harris, Marvin.1968. *The Rise of Anthropological Theory: A History of Theories of Culture*. London: Routledge & Kegan Paul.

Hobsbawm, Eric. 2017. *Primitive Rebels: Studies in Archaic Forms of Social Movement in the Nineteenth and Twentieth Centuries*. London: Abacus (first published as *Social Bandits and Primitive Rebels* in 1959).

Hobsbawm, Eric, and Terence Ranger (eds). 1983. *The Invention of Tradition*. Cambridge: Cambridge University Press.

Humphrey, Caroline. 1983. *Karl Marx Collective: Economy, Society and Religion in a Siberian Collective Farm*. Cambridge: Cambridge University Press.

Hunter (Wilson), Monica. 1936. *Reaction to Conquest: Effects of Contacts with Europeans on the Pondo of South Africa*. London: International African Institute.

Kapferer, Bruce. 2006. 'Situations, Crisis and the Anthropology of the Concrete: The Contribution of Max Gluckman', in T. Evens and D. Handelman (eds), *The Manchester School*. Oxford: Berghahn Books, 118–57.

Krige, Eileen. 1936. *The Social System of the Zulus*. London: Longman.

Kuper, Adam. 2015. *Anthropology and Anthropologists*, 4th edn. London: Routledge & Kegan Paul.

Kuper, Hilda. 1984. 'Function, History, Biography: Reflections on Fifty Years in the British Anthropological Tradition', in G.W. Stocking (ed.), *Functionalism Historicized: Essays on British Social Anthropology*, vol. 2. Madison: University of Wisconsin Press, 192–213.

Leach, Edmund. 1984. 'Glimpses of the Unmentionable in the History of British Social Anthropology'. *Annual Review of Anthropology* 13: 1–22.

Lewis, Herbert S. 2022. '*African Political Systems* and Political Anthropology', in Aleksandar Bošković and Günther Schlee (eds), *African Political Systems Revisited*. Oxford: Berghahn Books, 15–46.

Macmillan, Hugh. 1989. '"Paralyzed Conservatives": W.M. Macmillan, the Social Scientists, and "the Common Society", 1923–48', in Hugh Macmillan and Shula Marks (eds), *Africa and Empire: W.M. Macmillan, Historian and Social Critic*. Aldershot: Temple Smith for the Institute of Commonwealth Studies, University of London, 72–90.

———. 1995. 'Return to the Malungwana Drift: Max Gluckman, the Zulu Nation, and the Common Society'. *African Affairs* 94: 39–65.

————. 2000. 'From Race to Ethnic Identity: South Central Africa, Social Anthropology, and the Shadow of the Holocaust'. *Social Dynamics* 26(2): 87–115.

————. 2005. *An African Trading Empire: The Story of Susman Brothers & Wulfsohn, 1901–2005*. London: I.B. Tauris.

————. 2016. *Jack Simons: Teacher, Scholar, Comrade*. Auckland Park: Jacana Media.

Macmillan, Hugh, and Frank Shapiro. 2017. *Zion in Africa: The Jews of Zambia*, 2nd edn. London: I.B. Tauris.

Macmillan, W.M. 1938. *Africa Emergent*. London: Faber & Faber.

————. 1930. *Complex South Africa*. London: Faber & Faber.

————. 1975. *My South African Years*. Cape Town: David Philip.

Magubane, Bernard. 1971. 'A Critical Look at the Indices Used in the Measurement of Social Change in Colonial Africa'. *Current Anthropology* 12(4–5): 419–45.

Marks, Shula. 1986. *The Ambiguities of Dependence in South Africa: Class, Nationalism, and the State*. Johannesburg: Ravan Press.

Marx, Emanuel. 1975. 'Anthropological Studies in a Centralized State: The Bernstein Israel Research Project'. *Jewish Journal of Sociology* 17(2): 131–50.

Mayer, Philip, and Iona Mayer. 1961. *Townsmen or Tribesmen: Conservatism and the Process of Urbanization in a South African City*. Cape Town: Oxford University Press.

Mbikusita-Lewanika, Akashambatwa. 2021. *The Soul of the Barotse People: A Heritage of Land, Labour, Livelihood and Liberty*. Mongu: Barotse National Library, Documentary, Research and Development Services.

Mitchell, J. Clyde. 1958. *The Kalela Dance: Aspects of Social Relationship among Africans in Northern Rhodesia*. Manchester: Manchester University Press for RLI.

————. 1977. 'The Shadow of Federation, 1952–5'. *African Social Research* 24: 309–18.

Monckton Commission. 1960. *Advisory Committee on the Review of the Constitution of the Federation of Nyasaland*. Appendix VIII, Evidence. Volume 5. Part II. Written and Oral Evidence. London: HMSO. Cmd 1151-IV.

Money, Duncan. 2016. '"No Matter How Much or How Little They've Got, They Can't Settle Down": A Social History of Europeans on the Zambian Copperbelt, 1926–74', D.Phil. dissertation. Oxford: University of Oxford.

Moore, Sally Falk. 1978. 'Archaic Law and Modern Times on the Zambesi: Some Thoughts on Max Gluckman's Interpretation of Barotse Law', in

P.H. Gulliver (ed.), *Cross-Examinations: Essays in Memory of Max Gluck-man*. Leiden: Brill, 53–77.

Morrow, Seán. 2016. *The Fires Beneath: The Life of Monica Wilson, South African Anthropologist*. Cape Town: Penguin.

Murray, Bruce K. 1982. *Wits: The Early Years: A History of the University of Witwatersrand Johannesburg and its Precursors*. Johannesburg: Witwatersrand University Press.

Nader, Laura. 1988. 'The ADR Explosion: The Implications of Rhetoric in Legal Reform'. *Windsor Yearbook of Access to Justice*. Windsor: University of Windsor.

Pim, Sir Alan, and S. Milligan. 1938. *Report of the Commission Appointed to Enquire into the Financial and Economic Position of Northern Rhodesia*. London: HMSO.

Prins, Gwyn. 1980. *The Hidden Hippopotamus: Reappraisal in African History: The Early Colonial Experience in Western Zambia*. Cambridge: Cambridge University Press.

Radcliffe-Brown, A.R. 1923. 'The Methods of Ethnology and Social Anthropology'. *S.A. Journal of Science* 20: 124–47.

Reader, D.H. 1966. *Zulu Tribe in Transition: The Makhanya of Southern Natal*. Manchester: Manchester University Press.

Richards, Audrey. 1932. *Hunger and Work in a Savage Tribe: A Functional Study of Nutrition among the Southern Bantu*. London: Routledge.

———. 1939. *Land, Labour and Diet in Northern Rhodesia. An Economic Study of the Bemba Tribe*. London: Oxford University Press.

RLI. 1954. 'The Official Opening of the Rhodes-Livingstone Headquarters in Lusaka'. *Human Problems in British Central Africa* 16: 1–5.

Schapera, Isaac. 1938. 'Contact between European and Native in South Africa in Bechuanaland', in Lucy Mair (ed.), *Methods of Study of Culture Contact in Africa*. Oxford: Oxford University Press, 25–37.

Schumaker, Lyn, 2001. *Africanizing Anthropology: Fieldwork, Networks, and the Making of Cultural Knowledge in Central Africa*. Durham, NC: Duke University Press.

Shimoni, Gideon. 1980. *Jews and Zionism: The South African Experience, 1910–67*. Cape Town: Oxford University Press.

Shokeid, M. 2004. 'Max Gluckman and the Making of Israeli Anthropology'. *Ethnos* 69(20): 387–410.

Simons, Jack. 1977. 'Prologue'. *African Social Research* 24: 259–73.

Trapnell, Colin G., and J.N. Clothier. 1937. *The Soils, Vegetation and Agriculture of North-Western Rhodesia. Report of the Ecological Survey*. Lusaka: Government Pinter.

Turner, Edith. 2006. *Heart of Lightness*. Oxford: Berghahn Books.

Turner, Victor (ed.). 1971. *Colonialism in Africa. Volume 3. Profiles of Change: African Society and Colonial Rule.* Cambridge: Cambridge University Press.

University of Manchester. 1972. *Directory of Simon Visiting Professors and Fellows, 1944–70.* Manchester: University of Manchester.

Verdery, Katherine. 2003. *The Vanishing Hectare: Property and Value in Post-socialist Transylvania.* Ithaca: Cornell University Press.

Vilakazi, Absolom. 1965. *Zulu Transformations: A Study of the Dynamics of Social Change.* Pietermaritzburg: University of Natal Press.

Watson, William. 1958. *Tribal Cohesion in a Money Economy.* Manchester: Manchester University Press.

Werbner, Richard. 2020. *Anthropology after Gluckman: The Manchester School, Colonial and Postcolonial Transformations.* Manchester: Manchester University Press.

Wilson, Godfrey. 1941. *An Essay on the Economics of Detribalization in Northern Rhodesia* (Parts I and II). Livingstone: RLI.

Wilson, Monica. 1977. 'The First Three Years, 1938–4'. *African Social Research* 24: 279–83.

Wolpe, Harold. 1988. *Race, Class and the Apartheid State.* London: James Currey.

Worsley, Peter. 2008. *An Academic Skating on Thin Ice.* Oxford: Berghahn Books.

Yates, Ann, and Lewis Chester. 2006. *Michael Scott and His Lonely Struggle against Injustice.* London: Aurum Press.

INDEX

● ● ●